CW00547187

SHOW ME THE SCIENCE

Professor Luke O'Neill is a world-renowned immunologist and a professor of biochemistry at Trinity College Dublin. He is the author of four bestselling books, including *The Great Irish Science Book* for children. Luke is a member of the Royal Irish Academy and is a fellow of the Royal Society.

Tara O'Brien is an illustrator from Dublin, Ireland. Her work has a focus on diverse representations of people, body politics, mental health and our connection to nature.

Sheila Armstrong is a writer and editor from Sligo. She has worked on many children's books, including *The Great Irish Weather Book*, *The Great Irish Science Book*, *The Friendship Fairies* series and *What Makes Us Human*. She writes *The Great Big Irish Annual* series with Gill Books every year. She loves all things science and terrible jokes, and is positive she lost an electron around here somewhere.

SHOW ME
THE SCIENCE

A SCIENTIST'S GUIDE
TO LIFE'S BIGGEST QUESTIONS

PROFESSOR LUKE O'NEILL

ADAPTED BY SHEILA ARMSTRONG

GILL BOOKS

Gill Books
Hume Avenue
Park West
Dublin 12
www.gillbooks.ie

Gill Books is an imprint of M.H. Gill and Co.

9780717196128

Adapted by Sheila Armstrong from
*Nevermind the B#ll*cks, Here's the Science* by Luke O'Neill
Illustrations by Tara O'Brien
Designed by Graham Thew
Print origination by Sarah McCoy
Edited by Ciara McNee
Proofread by Jessica Spencer
Indexed by Kate Murphy
Printed by L.E.G.O. SpA, Italy
This book is typeset in Quasimoda.

The paper used in this book comes from the wood pulp
of sustainably managed forests.

A CIP catalogue record for this book is available from the British Library.

5 4 3 2 1

ACKNOWLEDGEMENTS

A big thank you to Sheila Armstrong, who did a superb job adapting *Never Mind the B#ll*cks, Here's the Science* into the book you are holding in your hand (or listening to or reading on your device). At least, I think it was Sheila, as opposed to ChatGPT … read on and see if you can tell!

CONTENTS

INTRODUCTION

Welcome to *Show Me the Science*! Strap yourself in and put on your serious thinking face – we're about to take a journey through some of the most difficult and exciting questions that we humans are facing today.

One of the most impressive things that our species, *Homo sapiens*, can do is think about thinking. We can have a thought, and then ask: Why did I have that thought? Why do I believe certain things? How do I know what's true? It can get pretty crowded in our brains, with all these thoughts rattling around and bouncing off each other. What's useful is to have a framework for sorting through these questions. This framework won't give us the answers, but it can teach us *how* to think, and how to get closer to the truth.

Enter science! The motto of the oldest scientific society in the world (the Royal Society) is *Nullius in verba*, which means *take nobody's word for it*. This means that we are all in charge of finding things out for ourselves. We shouldn't accept easy answers like 'Because it just is!' (I bet you've heard that one before.) Science is a fantastic tool – a way of seeing the world – that can help us *take nobody's word for it*. It starts as the simplest and most important thing in the world: an idea. To test that idea, scientists come up with experiments, which give them lots of juicy data. Based on that data, they come up with a theory. That theory is checked by other scientists, who hopefully come up with the same results. If they don't get the same results, they go back and look at the theory again. But if they keep getting the same answers, they start to think:

hey, there might be something there. But that's not enough! They have to test it again and again, looking at all the angles, making sure that nothing has been overlooked.

Scientists are cautious, careful people – if you tell them the sky is blue, they'll ask you to prove it.[1] They are also very competitive and love having scientific arguments. They are always trying to prove each other wrong, and sometimes things can get quite testy. But when they work together, they are unbeatable. The best scientists just want one simple thing: the truth. But it's not easy to get there, and there can be a lot of false trails.

Scientists obsess about the connection between cause and effect. Or, to put it another way, the link between correlation and causation. The correlation/causation issue is critical in science: something might happen at the same time as something else (correlation), but that doesn't mean that one thing is the *cause* of the other. An example of how the two can get mixed up is a study which showed a correlation between the number of babies being born and the number of storks nesting nearby. The investigators found that there was a correlation, and the statistics backed it up. This shows us that storks bring babies, right? Not so fast. When the investigators looked more closely,

---

1 Easy. Sunlight reaches Earth's atmosphere and is scattered in all directions by all the gases and particles in the air. Blue light travels as shorter, smaller waves, so it is scattered more than the other colours. This is why we see a blue sky. Next question!

they found that the reason for the correlation was that storks were nesting near larger villages (which had more chimneys for them to build nests on), where the number of newborn babies was greater. So even though there was a correlation, it wasn't because the storks were delivering the babies. The correlation was actually with the size of the village! The bigger the village, the more chimneys; the more chimneys, the more storks, but also the more babies being born. This study shows us that we shouldn't jump to conclusions.[2]

Jumping to conclusions, accepting easy answers and making snap decisions are the enemies of science. So are anecdotes – just because your mother's brother's nephew's postman told you something, it doesn't mean it is true. This is why the internet can be so dangerous. As the saying goes, a lie can travel around the world and back again while the truth is still lacing up its boots. Believing fake news is due to lazy thinking (you can just hear your teacher saying that, can't you?). Science is the antidote to fake news, so we need it now more than ever.

---

2 But you never know, it could be true – and, as a scientist, I must remain open-minded (and slightly crazy) to even consider the possibility. The most important scientists were often a bit mad – Marie Sklowdawska Curie kept a tube of deadly radium beside her bed as a nightlight.

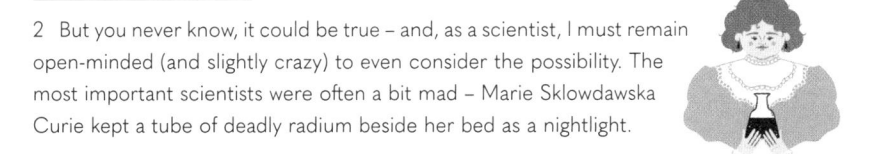

QUESTION EVERYTHING

Asking questions is how we understand the world and our place in it. Questions like:

- Do we have control over our lives?
- Why do we do things that are bad for us?
- Why do we believe in things we can't see?
- What's the difference between men and women?
- Are we alone in the universe?

Before we answer, we need experiments, data, statistics and a lot of thought. But the media wants quick, snappy answers, so they can print articles with headlines like: CATS ARE ACTUALLY DOGS WITH LONGER WHISKERS or ORANGE JUICE WILL MAKE YOUR LEGS DROP OFF or LONELY GHOSTS ARE JUST LOOKING FOR HUGS. Politicians want easy answers so they can go to the voters and say, 'Everything's fine! Just vote for me again.' This is where the problems can begin.

People don't really want to know that scientists are sceptical or doubtful. They want scientists to be *sure* about things. But slow and careful thought is key to science: it helps us see where the truth is, instead of just doing what *feels* right. Humans tend to do this, so we have to be careful. It feels right that the prince and princess live happily ever after in their beautiful castle. We don't want to hear about the castle's electricity bills or the rowdy neighbours who overfill their bins. Stories are simple, but the truth is complex. The great thing about how science works is that it can strip away the fantasy, through testing and retesting, arguing and debating, deleting and changing.

This book is about the science behind the biggest issues that we are facing today. These issues fascinate me, and hopefully you. Using my scientific training, I've examined the science behind some of the questions you might have about how our world works. I try to answer them with data and/or experiments (science loves both of these). I've done my best to give you the best evidence to support my conclusions. You might want to check the facts yourself, and that's fine. At the end of each chapter, I give my own bottom line. You could be lazy and just read these, because they summarise what each chapter is about. Or you could do the right thing and dig deeper to find out the science that led me to my conclusions.

I hope the book helps and informs you as you grow and decide your own opinions on these important issues. I hope you come away positive about your own life if the topics are especially relevant to you. Some may make you feel uneasy. Humans are built to be uneasy – it's in our nature. But it's only by talking about things that we make progress. True wisdom is knowing that you don't know everything, but still trying to learn as much as possible.

Most of all, I hope you feel more prepared for the future – a future we are all headed towards, with science as our one true friend and travelling companion. Science isn't good or bad, and it doesn't belong to anyone in particular. It is not a religion or a political system – it is a way of thinking that can help us understand the wonderful, bizarre, terrifying, mind-boggling mysteries of our world. With science, we can navigate our way through really important questions. And you will soon see why we should always be questioning, always trying to work things out, always saying: show me the science.

CHAPTER 1

DO WE HAVE CONTROL OVER OUR LIVES?

Y OU PROBABLY THINK you're reading this book because you chose to. You probably think you're free to do whatever you want. You go through your life looking at your options and deciding what to do: I'll have pizza for dinner. I'll support Shamrock Rovers. I'll study French instead of German. I'll drop out of school, live in a yurt and stop showering. It seems like we are in control of our own destiny. And yet, when you scratch the surface, it's not quite so simple.

The idea of free will is the idea that we can make any choices we like. We all have a strong sense of freedom, which makes us believe that we can do whatever we want in life. But free will is one of those ideas that tie philosophers up in knots.[1] Some philosophers say that we only *think* we have free will – that everything we say, do and believe is down to the conditions that we live in; that we have no control over our future at all. Others think the whole idea of free will is ridiculous: a lot of what happens to us happens by chance,

---

1 Philosophers study knowledge and the nature of reality. They spend their days arguing about big ideas, coming up with theories and writing long, complex papers. Unlike scientists, who do the same thing, but with microscopes.

instead of us deciding to do things. And anyway, if free will is real, surely we would make better decisions?[2] Why would we choose to do silly things, like eating that third slice of cake, buying those diamond-encrusted sunglasses, or following that interesting bird into the middle of a busy motorway? Many philosophers have got into some pretty heated arguments over these ideas. Some have probably lost the (free) will to keep thinking about it.

And so, science enters the fight. Time to roll up our sleeves and set those philosophers straight. The great thing about science is that it allows you to predict the future, *if* you know where you are starting from. If you fire a cannonball of a particular weight, with a particular force, you can predict, using maths, exactly where it will land after you've fired it. In other words, if we know the rules of the game, everything that follows – even our own complex human lives – should be predictable.

But, as we'll find out, it's not quite that simple.

---

2 See Chapter 4 for more on terrible decisions.

GENE MACHINE

So, how do we make decisions in our day-to-day lives?

First, a lot comes down to our genetic makeup – the hard-wired information that is passed down to us from our parents. There are variants of genes that affect everything about us, from how good we are at sports to what foods we like, and these will change our behaviour. Genes passed down by your parents may even influence how often you poo! Did you know that there are genes that make some people hate the taste of coriander? So if you are one of those people, choosing an Italian takeaway instead of a Mexican one is still a choice, but it's one that is influenced by your genetics. Speaking of takeaways: whether or not we're hungry can affect our decisions. A Swedish study demonstrated that hungry rats are much more impulsive – which means doing things without thinking. As the saying goes, you're not yourself when you're hungry.

Then there's our upbringing. If children are raised in a certain way, they will turn into adults with certain characteristics. For example, children who cooperate with their friends and who are helpful to others are far more likely to get a college degree by the age of 25. So your primary school teachers were right: sharing is caring (and no, that doesn't mean sharing exam answers). If you have family and teachers who encourage you, you are also more likely to go to college. This is called the Pygmalion effect – if people expect you to do well, you are more likely to do well.

And our environment makes a huge difference. For example, if you are part of a religious community with strict laws, like the

Amish community in the USA, you will probably grow up to lead a life that fits with those laws. You will marry another Amish person. You will never own a car or a smartphone. Could you imagine?! In the same way, there probably aren't many bobsleigh champions in Jamaica, as you'll know if you've ever seen the film *Cool Runnings*. Do Jamaican sportspeople have the free will to follow their snowy dreams? Sure! Do they have the right tools, opportunities, or the perfect environment to practise in? Maybe not so much. Still, the Jamaican bobsleigh team is still going strong, and they competed in the 2022 Winter Olympics. So while parts of our lives might be set in stone, there's no telling what's possible.

PROBLEM PARASITES

But what if you had a parasite in your body that was controlling you? Making you act differently? It sounds like something from a zombie movie, but it could be real.

Toxoplasma gondii is a common parasite in cats. It infects the brains of billions of species all over the world, including humans, but it particularly loves to hang out in furry felines. Once a person or animal is infected (from the poo of the cat, or from eating an infected animal), the parasite can stay in their body for life. When mice become infected, something odd happens:

their behaviour changes. They become more reckless and are actually attracted to the smell of cats, which usually ends badly for the mouse. Charles Darwin, the father of evolution, would love this example – a complex relationship between three species: cat, mouse and parasite. The mouse's behaviour has been changed to make sure the parasite gets to the cat – and also gives the cat a tasty snack.

Humans infected with *toxoplasma* are more likely to be aggressive. There are different amounts of infection in different countries: around 7 per cent of Irish people are infected, but 67 per cent of Brazilians are. Men and women respond differently to the infection, too: men become less afraid of risk but more narrow-minded, while women become more outgoing. This is a sneaky way that a parasite can change our behaviour. *Toxoplasma* can also be very dangerous for people who are pregnant or have a weak immune system. So, to avoid this pesky parasite, remember to wash your hands next time you're changing the kitty litter.

Ophiocordyceps unilateralis, also known by the much more fun name of 'zombie-ant fungus', is another example of this type of control. When this fungus infects an ant, it hijacks its mind. It forces the ant to leave the safety of its nest and climb a nearby plant, where it makes the ant lock its jaws around a leaf. The ant is stuck there and eventually dies. Then the fungus sends a long stalk through the ant's head, which grows into a ball full of spores. When the ball bursts, the spores rain down on other ants below, zombifying them in turn.

You might think what you're doing is based on your own free will, but in reality you could be the pawn of a zombie parasite in your brain. Brains? Braaaains …

PLAYING THE ODDS

When something unusual happens to us, we often say, 'What are the odds of that happening?' We are often amazed by coincidences or apparently random events in our lives: 'If I hadn't missed the school bus I would have had to do that surprise geography test' or 'If I hadn't gone to that football match, I wouldn't have met the coach who picked me for the Irish team.' But these things may not be as strange as you think. We are amazed by coincidence because we don't really understand probability – how likely something is to happen.

If you meet someone with the same birthday as you, you might say, 'Wow! That's a huge coincidence!' There are 365 days in a year,

365 possible birthdays, so the probability of the two of you having the same one is 1 in 365. But here's an interesting piece of maths: how many people need to be in a room for there to be a 50/50 chance that two will have the same birthday? The answer is 23 people, which looks like a tiny number. But there are almost eight billion people on Earth and, since there are so many of us, there is a large probability of really unlikely things happening somewhere. The odds of winning the Euromillions lotto are 1 in 139,838,160. If lots of people buy a lotto ticket, one will win – no surprise there. The surprise is only for the person who wins.[3]

Then there's the story of Violet Jessop: she was on three famous ships that sank and survived every time. Violet was on board the *Olympic* when it crashed into HMS *Hawke* in 1911. The following year, 1912, she survived the sinking of the *Titanic*. Then, in 1916, she survived the sinking of the *Britannic*. How could this be? Surely the probability of one woman being in three of the most famous sinkings in history is teeny tiny? It is, until you learn that she was a nurse who worked for the White Star Line and was working on all of these three ships.

What all this means is that surprising things can happen to you based on random probability, but you can still tweak the odds in your favour. Joining a football club will make it more likely that you will play for Ireland. Doing the lotto will make it more likely that you will win €1,000,000. Both *seem* to involve you acting on your free will, but they really don't. You sign up for the football team because

---

3 But if you *do* happen to win big, don't forget about a certain professor who explained all about probability.

all your friends are doing it. You do the lotto because the adverts are aimed at you and you think you might have a chance.

Which leads us to another way your free will is tweaked by the world around you …

ATTACK OF THE ADS

We see them everywhere: at bus stops, before movies, on social media, in newspapers, on billboards. And the reason we see advertising everywhere is because it *works*. Advertisers try to change the way you think, or change your mind about something, so that they can get their hands on your hard-earned cash. They try to make their products look good, perhaps even better than they really are. And this works: if you give young children exactly the same foods, they will say that the ones in the McDonald's wrapper taste better. Why? Because they've seen ads that tell them just how yummy that Big Mac is. One person who used to work in advertising and now works on banning fast food advertising said that 'junk food advertising has become a monster, manipulating young people's emotions and their choices'. So far, there are no rules about advertising junk food in Ireland. Eating too much fat and sugar can even cause behavioural changes, including being more impulsive – doing things on the spur of the moment – which is likely to lead to yet more bad decision-making.

The fact that we live so much of our lives online is making the influence of those ads even sneakier. Facebook, Google and other sites collect information on us and then sell it to advertisers, who use it to target likely customers. This is a good thing, right? You like surfing, so you're shown ads about the latest in wetsuits and suncream. Well, not quite, as it turns out. Advertisers can find out all kinds of things about you – things you might not want them to know (such as, say, your secret love for cold baked bean sandwiches).

You accidentally reveal an awful lot about yourself on social media, including your personality traits and the things you agree with. An algorithm (a set of rules in a computer program) can learn from this information and use it to manipulate you. This is really important for democracy and elections. Many companies have used online campaigns to persuade people to vote in a certain way. So, for example, a website knows that you spend all day searching for omelette recipes. The algorithm sends you ads for a political party that says they will give everyone a free chicken. You decide to vote for them because, hey, more eggs means more omelettes! This is worrying, because we might not even see that it is happening. It's difficult to know what to do about all this, but being aware of it is the first step towards fighting it. If you're being shown an ad for something, it's worth thinking about why you're seeing it.

We are also letting the little machines that we carry around in our pocket control our lives. We *seem* to have control over this (just turn it off!), yet many of us are addicted to our phones and check them constantly, even when we should be asleep. An amazing 40 per cent of teenagers say they check their phones twice *during* the night! Our phones give us access to a huge amount of information. But

our brains weren't built to handle all this information – we evolved to live in small groups and remember information about our close friends and family. Now we can find out every time a celebrity clips his toenails or our great-aunt finds a funny-shaped vegetable. All that information is making us think and behave in ways that we might not even recognise. If we want to be truly free to make our own decisions, we'll have to lose the chains that keep us locked to our screens.

WRITTEN IN THE STARS

Finally, when it comes to the directions our lives take, there are things like horoscopes, fortune-telling, tarot cards, psychics and personality tests. These all claim to tell us something about the future based on who we are, when we were born or how we are feeling. Many people swear by them and believe they are true. But are they?

In a famous experiment, a psychologist gave his students a personality test and told them they would be getting individual, personalised feedback based on their answers. The psychologist read over their answers and gave them a list of 13 personal comments. Almost all the students thought their feedback was true to their personality – they rated it 4.3 on a scale of 0 (very poor) to 5 (excellent). So what was the problem? They were all given the exact same feedback, based on an astrology magazine the tester had picked up! This is something called the Barnum Effect, named after the infamous showman and trickster P.T. Barnum (played by Hugh Jackman in *The Greatest Showman*), who supposedly said 'there's a sucker born every minute'. We often believe that general statements about our own lives and personalities are true. This is why horoscopes and personality quizzes are so popular. We take the information that matches what we think about ourselves and ignore all the bits that don't fit – of course Scorpios are hot-tempered (except when they're calm), and of course Leos are confident (except when they're shy).

Cold reading, a technique used by psychics and fortune tellers, is another example of this. Cold reading combines high-probability guesses and broad statements with clever language and psychological tricks. For example:

- 'You are sometimes shy, especially with people you've just met.'
- 'You can be hard on yourself.'
- 'You like things to be fair.'
- 'You're having problems with a close friend.'

Do any of these sound like you? Statements like these make it seem like the psychic has amazing insight or paranormal gifts. They might get something wrong, but our brains will ignore that and focus on the things they got right. A good cold reader is a good listener and observer who carefully studies an audience to gather information. You'd be amazed at how much they can learn about you just from body language, such as the way you sit, or the way you talk, or even just your clothes or hairstyle.

The truth is, unfortunately, that psychics can't predict the future, and your personality isn't written in the stars. In fact, your life is influenced by random probabilities in a universe that is cold and unpredictable. Or by the Great Algorithm in the Sky. Cheerful, isn't it?

THE RIGHT CHOICE

It's not always easy to know what the right choice is. Psychologists say that before making a decision, you should keep a few things in mind. First, sleep on it: this will give you a better perspective. Second, never make a decision if you are feeling overwhelmed or tired. Third, it's probably best to make a decision on a full stomach – remember those hungry, impulsive rats? We need to use logic and facts to help us make the right decisions in all areas of our lives, rather than giving in and feeling powerless. That's what the algorithm wants you to do!

Whatever about the decisions we make, many things in our lives are definitely beyond our control – illnesses, loss of loved ones, accidents. We can, of course, try to limit the risk of some of these things happening by looking after our health and following advice from experts. You're less likely to be struck by lightning if you don't go golfing in a thunderstorm.

But there's no point in stressing about what the future may bring. Some scientists believe in parallel universes, where every decision leads to two or more alternative universes. The author Terry Pratchett called this idea the Trousers of Time – every time you make a decision, the future splits off into two timelines, or trouserlegs, and you continue down these paths. One version of you got the chocolate ice cream, another version got the strawberry. So why worry? You might be living lots of alternative lives somewhere else. Hopefully, somewhere out there, there's a version of you that has ten pairs of trousers with pockets full of ice cream.

The bottom line: Take your time making decisions, look out for outside influences and use your brain. Now, keep reading. Go on, go on, go on – you know you want to.

CHAPTER 2

WHERE DO WE GET MEDICINES FROM?

I SPEND A LOT of my working life doing medical research. I work on inflammation, a process that protects us from harm and fixes our bodies when they are damaged. The problem is, our bodies can be both our best friends and our worst enemies. Inflammation can sometimes turn on us and give us painful diseases like rheumatoid arthritis, Crohn's disease, multiple sclerosis and Parkinson's disease. All these diseases involve our bodies becoming inflamed and badly damaged, with symptoms of that damage being all too real.

The good news is that we are making progress in finding medicines to treat these diseases. Look at what happened with COVID-19 – we quickly developed and tested a lot of new vaccines and drugs. This shows us that when we are faced with a crisis, scientists and drug developers can put a huge amount of effort into finding a solution. It's a slow business, but there is hope.

The future of medicine looks promising for all of us. Hundreds of thousands of scientists and doctors have been working for decades with one goal in mind: to find new treatments or to come up with ways to prevent diseases in the first place. Right now, new drugs are being approved for a range of diseases. With many more in the pipeline, all kinds of treatments – new tablets, injections, gene modifications, even organ replacements – are now within reach.

SAINTLY SOLUTIONS

In ancient times, before we had any scientific understanding of diseases, people struggled to understand how illnesses seemed to be so random. You might have got sick while your next-door neighbour stayed healthy. Did someone put a curse on you? Did the gods do it because you were a bad person? All kinds of superstitions shot up to try to keep illness at bay. Old Irish folklore said you should tie a bunch of mint around your wrist to keep infection away. If someone died of a fever, a flock of sheep should be run through the house to protect the other people in the house.[1] Our ancestors also looked to the saints for protection: the first medical specialists.

- St Blaise was the patron saint of sore throats (and of wool combers, who might have suffered from sore throats from all that tickly wool).
- St Christina the Astonishing (she must have been great) was the patron saint of mental illness.
- St Ursicinus was the patron saint for a stiff neck (which you might get from trying to pronounce his name).
- St Expeditus was the patron saint of procrastination (I prayed to him regularly while I wrote this book).

The ancient Greeks believed in four humours (another word for fluid): blood, phlegm, yellow bile and black bile. This wasn't some disgusting cocktail, but the four liquids that they thought make up the human body. If these humours were out of balance, a person would get sick. For example, if someone had a fever, they had too much blood in their body, so logically, the patient should be 'bled'

---

1 But only if it was really baaaaaad.

to get rid of the extra blood. Then there was Asclepius, the Greek god of medicine. Many people went to his temples to sleep, hoping to be cured in their dreams. In fairness, who hasn't felt better after a good nap? A Greek doctor called Hippocrates caused a stir when he suggested that diseases could have natural rather than supernatural causes. He also came up with a code of conduct for physicians which is still used worldwide, and he is now known as the father of modern medicine.

The Romans had some interesting beliefs too. Cato the Elder prescribed cabbage as a treatment for many ailments ranging from constipation to deafness. Another Roman, Pliny the Elder, had a host of cures. Funnily enough, a lot of them involved dung – goat, pig, bird and even human. Others included 'earthworms, boiled in oil and injected into the ear on the side affected' for toothache, 'a camel's brain, dried and taken in vinegar' for epilepsy, and a glue made of 'the ears and genitals of the bull', for burns.[2] These early medicines might seem silly now, but the Romans weren't stupid – they also knew that dirty drinking water and sewage can lead to disease. They built aqueducts to bring clean water into towns and had public lavatories with streams running underneath them to carry away waste.

2 Pliny the Elder died the day Mount Vesuvius destroyed Pompeii. Pliny went to investigate the eruption, with a pillow tied to his head to protect him. His curiosity proved fatal.

Doctors in the Middle Ages were a bit better at diagnosis: they used observation, felt the patient's pulse, and looked at their urine. However, most people never saw a doctor. They were treated by the local wise woman, or the barber-surgeon, who pulled out rotten teeth, set broken bones and applied leeches (leeches were used to suck out a person's blood, which was thought to prevent illness and cure disease). Monks and nuns also ran hospitals in their monasteries, which took in the sick and dying. This was the first time that medicine became available to all, not just those who could pay for it.

Around the end of the eighteenth century, more people began to live in cities, which led to cramped and dirty conditions. Diseases like cholera and typhoid were common. Many people, including the famous nurse Florence Nightingale, believed that 'miasmas', or bad air, were responsible. This helped make a connection between bad sanitation – polluted drinking water and poor sewage disposal – and disease, but it wasn't until later that the true cause would be discovered.

Some doctors had suspected that invisible organisms might cause disease, but it wasn't until the experiments of Louis Pasteur in the nineteenth century that the idea of 'germ theory' became accepted. After that, scientists quickly began to identify which germs cause which diseases, and how best to treat them. In 1928, Alexander Fleming noticed a stray mould on a culture of bacteria in his laboratory. This mould was penicillin, and it became the first antibiotic. After that, doctors were sucking diesel, and new discoveries came fast and furious.

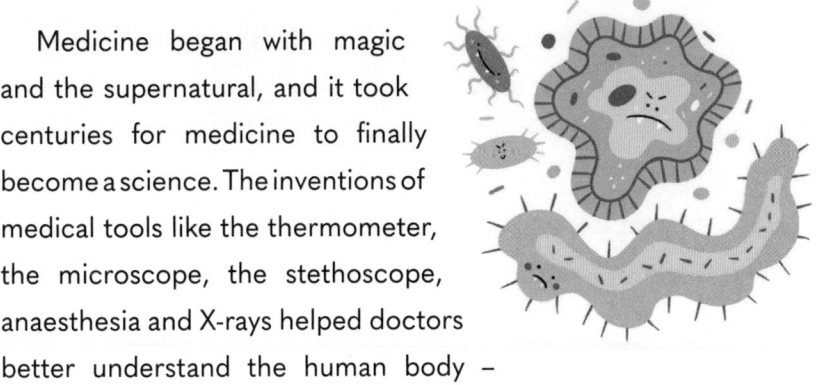

Medicine began with magic and the supernatural, and it took centuries for medicine to finally become a science. The inventions of medical tools like the thermometer, the microscope, the stethoscope, anaesthesia and X-rays helped doctors better understand the human body – and helped patients stay alive, or even better, recover. There was a lot of ignorance mixed with huge leaps forward, thanks to clever men and women who asked the simple question: How can I make this sick person better?

DRUGGED UP

As we've just learned, natural remedies have always played a big part in medicine. It might be fun to sneer at some of the stranger ones (looking at you, Pliny the Elder), but many of these ancient cures were right on the mark. A Sumerian (Middle Eastern) clay tablet from about 2100 BCE mentions using the poppy plant as a medicine. In 1804, a German pharmacist used the same poppy plant to create a strong painkiller – morphine.[3] An Egyptian hieroglyph (a form of early writing) from 1550 BCE mentions an anti-inflammatory plant that was used to treat eye inflammation and haemorrhoids

---

3 It worked a little too well and people became addicted – see Chapter 4 for more(phine).

(piles). What was that plant? Marijuana, which we now know contains cannabinoids, substances that suppress inflammation. In 1899, the drug company Bayer launched a new drug which came from chemicals in willow bark. Willow had been known for centuries to have anti-inflammatory properties. The leaves and bark of the willow have been mentioned in ancient texts from Assyria, Sumer and Egypt. Bayer gave it a new name that you might be familiar with: aspirin.

While some drugs have been discovered using clues from nature, most of the medicines we use nowadays have been created in labs. Scientists can extract chemicals that work and mix them with others to make an effective drug, whether it comes as a liquid, a pill or an injection. But discovering a new medicine involves scientists with lots of specialities, depending on the disease, including – take a deep breath – immunology, biochemistry, genetics, neuroscience, molecular biology, pharmacology, bioinformatics and cell biology, to name but a few. Then there are the chemists (who make the drugs), doctors (also of many specialities) and the specialists and regulators who make sure everything is done properly. As they say, it takes a village.

It's not a short process, either. It takes around twelve years to get from the research lab to the patient. The drug-discovery part takes the most time. This is when companies either find a new target in a disease to fire a drug at, or work on one discovered by someone else and then make a medicine to target it. This stage usually involves testing the new medicine in animals, which are given a specific disease that has similar features to the disease in humans. There are so-called animal models of many diseases, including cancer, arthritis, inflammatory bowel disease and neurodegenerative diseases (diseases that attack the nervous system). A lot of people don't agree with using animals to test medicines.[4] At the moment we have to use animal testing to meet government rules for most drugs, but we are gradually learning how to use human tissues and cells instead. This pre-clinical phase (before drugs can be used on humans) can take anything from three years to twenty years and can cost millions or even billions of dollars.

Once a company has a new medicine, it has to be approved by the drugs authority. In the USA this is the Food and Drug Administration (FDA). The FDA was set up in 1906 to make sure that food and drugs on sale in the USA are as safe as possible – partly because of an incident in 1902 when a vaccine for diphtheria killed 13 children in St Louis, Missouri. The FDA was given powers to decide which drugs are safe and whether they should be used only under the supervision of a medical professional. The European equivalent of the FDA is the European Medicines Agency (EMA). The FDA and the EMA have to give their approval for any new drug to be tested in clinical trials and, more important, to be used in the USA or Europe.

Before these agencies were set up, you could add anything you liked to food or medicine. In 1933, the FDA set up a travelling exhibition nicknamed the Chamber of Horrors. It showed off some

---

4 We owe a lot to animals when it comes to discoveries in medicine. See Chapter 3 for the most important cow in medical history.

of the dangerous, deceptive and just plain useless products on the market. Highlights included:

- A jam called Bred-Spred that didn't contain any fruit, just artificial colours, flavours and fake strawberry seeds
- A hair-removing product that was actually rat poison
- Mascara that caused blindness and foundation that was full of dangerous mercury
- Radioactive water – which, to be fair, was exactly what it said it was. That didn't stop it from being deadly.

Nowadays, thankfully, food and medicines have to be clearly labelled with all the ingredients they contain.

But how do we make sure a drug is safe in the first place? The FDA sets out three phases of clinical trials, which is considered the safest way to do things. Phase 1 is only about safety – researchers want to learn if the drug is safe, what amount is safe, and if there are any side effects. If all seems well, the researchers move on to the next stage. Phase 2 is the first time the drug is tested in patients with the disease, and it usually involves tens of patients and tens of 'controls'. A control is a person who is given a different drug, or no drug at all. The use of controls is important, because it helps researchers decide if any changes are due to the actual drug being used. Phase 3 is a repeat of Phase 2 but consists of a lot more patients, sometimes thousands in the treated group and thousands in the control group. If all is well with Phase 3, the drug will be approved for the market. Finally, after the drug has started being used, the company will see what's happening with the patients who are taking the new medicine. This is Phase 4. A new medicine can fail at any phase of this complex and time-consuming process, and just 5–10 per cent of drugs tested make it to patients.

Drug companies and patients often feel that the FDA takes too long to approve a drug. Sometimes, this process can be speeded up. If there is a public health emergency, like the COVID-19 pandemic, the FDA can grant emergency approvals. Scientists had a head start in this case, as the technologies used in the COVID-19 vaccines have been in development for many years to fight similar viruses, and research into how to respond to a pandemic began long before COVID-19. The development of these vaccines was also speeded up thanks to huge amounts of funding and lots of scientists, manufacturers and distributors working together. And because so many people were infected with COVID-19, trials could be run very quickly. Importantly, safety monitoring continues even after vaccines and drugs have been approved, allowing warnings and information about any potential rare side effects to be made publicly available.

PAYING THE PRICE

Considering this long and complex process, what is the actual cost of developing a new medicine, from drug discovery through clinical trials to approval? Unsurprisingly, it's a lot. An awful lot. The average cost of getting a drug to market is $2.6 billion. Compare that with the first iPhone, which cost 'only' $150 million to develop. Buckingham Palace is estimated to be worth more than $1.4 billion. So if you want to make money, either get into electronics or join the Royal Family.

But someone has to pay for all this hard work. Taxpayers pay for a lot of this research, but we also rely on philanthropists (people who give money to good causes), charities and drug companies. All that effort eventually delivers what we all want – a new medicine that works on a particular disease. Many of these new medicines will emerge in the coming years. But having spent so much money on developing a drug, how much can a drug company charge for a new treatment?

For a new medicine, pricing begins with the drug company estimating its value. A blockbuster first-in-class treatment (which means a brand new drug for a major disease, not a lookalike of something that's already out there) will be set at a high price. Once a drug company sets the price, it can be bargained over, a bit like haggling at a market stall. Health insurers, pharmacies and governments (like the HSE in Ireland) all get involved. And constant monitoring is also needed – whatever about new drugs arriving to the market, drug companies can also raise the price of drugs already on the market. Politics, corruption and good old-fashioned greed can make this more likely. An example is a company called Mylan, which raised the price of its EpiPen by 500 per cent, from just under $100 to more than $600. The EpiPen is used to save the lives of people who are having a major allergic reaction. Thanks to angry reactions from the public and media, that price has come down.

But there are other issues to think about. Some health systems, like the NHS in the UK, are free. In the USA, there is a complicated system of insurance that often means people end up with high medical bills. In the developing world, many people don't have access to much medical care at all. How do we make sure everyone can get what they need? Health organisations like the HSE only have a limited amount of money. If they spend lots of money on a small number of patients with certain diseases, does that mean there will be less for other areas where more people might benefit? Governments have to decide how to spend their budget, and it can be difficult when there are new and expensive medicines. Is it better to treat ten slightly sick people or one very sick person? These questions don't have obvious answers. This is the tricky, frustrating and difficult field of medical ethics. These people stay up all night worrying about these problems so we don't have to!

ONWARDS AND UPWARDS

There are also exciting things happening in new medical technology. Gene therapy is fixing faulty genes in the very blueprints of our bodies. Soon, we could be growing new organs in vats or 3D-printing liver replacements. People are testing how to use drones to deliver medical supplies to remote or dangerous areas. Robotic doctors could be walking the hospital halls.[5] Every year, more than two million research papers are published – far too many for any individual scientist to read – but machines don't get bored or lose focus. BenevolentAI has created algorithms that read research papers, clinical trial results and other sources of medical information in search of previously overlooked relationships between genes, drugs and disease. Let's just hope it stays benevolent!

The bottom line: Whatever way you look at it, there are exciting and challenging times ahead for all of us. Tough decisions will have to be made. Ultimately, the end goal is creating new treatments that can benefit everyone, not just those who can afford to pay.

---

5   See Chapter 13 for more on where we're headed. There'll be more robots, I promise.

CHAPTER 3

SHOULD WE ALL GET VACCINATED?

IMAGINE THERE IS a disease that you can catch from a swimming pool. A disease so dangerous and sneaky that one day you have a headache, and then you are paralysed – your arms, legs and body stop working. To breathe, you have to lie inside a tube-shaped machine called an iron lung. Swimming pools, bars, bowling alleys and churches all close to stop the spread of this disease. Streets are sprayed with pesticides in case insects are carrying the sickness. Drivers won't pump up their tyres, afraid of bringing infected air home with them. Some people even refuse to talk on the phone in case the disease could be passed on that way.

Does this sound like something from a horror movie? Well, it was pretty horrible alright, but it really happened. The disease was polio, and it infected hundreds of thousands of children every year. People weren't quite sure how it worked, so they believed some strange things about how it was passed on or treated.[1] It was a terrifying time.

But along came hope. In the 1950s, scientists managed to develop a weapon to fight this disease and began to send it out into the world. Before this weapon, there were around 15,000–20,000 cases of paralytic polio in the USA every year. Afterwards, that number fell to fewer than ten – not ten thousand, TEN. What exactly was this weapon? A vaccine against the virus that causes polio.

---

1 You might laugh at the idea of a disease spreading through phones, but during the COVID-19 pandemic, many cures were suggested, including: drinking cow urine, exorcisms through your TV, eating poisonous fruit, USB flash drives ... the list goes on.

THAT POXY JAB

After living through the COVID-19 pandemic, you're probably sick of hearing about vaccines. But seeing as they are humanity's single most effective medical weapon, it's worth hearing a little bit more. To put it simply, vaccines are a preventive treatment that gives us immunity to disease. The word 'immunity' comes from the Latin word *immunis*, meaning 'exemption'. In Roman times, this usually meant an exemption from paying taxes, which was given to certain Roman citizens (for example, soldiers returning home).[2] In the case of infectious diseases, immunity means an exemption from getting the disease. This is also where the word 'immunology' comes from. It's the medical study of our body's own protective immune systems.

Clever people down through the years noticed that after someone got sick from a disease, they rarely got it again. The person who was sick became exempt. The clever people used this knowledge to develop treatments, which eventually brought us to vaccines. This is a brilliant example of the scientific method: people made an observation, did tests, and came up with a theory.

The history of one terrible disease shows us exactly how this happened. Smallpox was highly contagious. One-third of people who got it died; another third were badly scarred; and the final third were unharmed because their immune systems managed to fight it off. In ancient Rome, an outbreak of smallpox killed 10 million

---

2 Then again, some historians suggest that Roman soldiers were sometimes paid in salt. It's where the word 'salary' comes from. Imagine paying your taxes by handing over a salt-shaker to the government. Keep the change …

people, or 10 per cent of the population of the Roman Empire. In cities like Rome the death toll was as high as 33 per cent.

People were desperate to figure out how to stop smallpox, and they had an inkling about how to do just that. A ninth-century Islamic physician described how exposure to smallpox gave lasting immunity. Around 1000 CE, the Chinese began using dried crusts from skin lesions (scabs) of patients with smallpox. How did they use them? Well, they inhaled them. Better than sprinkling them on your breakfast cereal, I suppose. Some cultures like India and East Africa used 'inoculation', which meant using a needle to put the crusty bits under a person's skin. In England in 1721, Lady Mary Wortley Montagu gave seven prisoners who were going to be executed the chance to try inoculation instead. All seven survived and were released. Sounds like a good deal, but it was risky – in some cases, this type of inoculation actually *gave* people smallpox, because it could contain live infectious virus.

In 1798 Edward Jenner, a doctor in Gloucestershire, England, tried a far safer method. Lots of people had noticed that milkmaids, who worked with cows, rarely got smallpox. Could this be because they often caught the much milder disease of cowpox? Jenner thought so – but he had to prove it. He scraped pus from blisters on the hands of a milkmaid who had caught cowpox from a cow called Blossom.[3]

---

3 Of course, Blossom got none of the credit. Her skin is now on the wall of a medical school in London. No good deed goes unpunished.

He inoculated an eight-year-old boy with the pus, which gave the boy a mild fever. When the boy was exposed to an inoculum – a tiny piece of infectious material – of smallpox, he didn't show any symptoms at all. With this experiment, Jenner had shown that cowpox could be used to protect from the much worse disease of smallpox. He treated over twenty more patients, including his 11-month-old son.

Following Jenner's success, many other vaccines were developed. In the 1880s, French scientist Louis Pasteur introduced vaccines for chicken cholera and anthrax, infectious farm animal diseases. In honour of Jenner, he used the term 'vaccination', from the Latin *vacca*, meaning 'cow' (thanks again, Blossom). Other vaccines soon followed: in 1884 for rabies, in 1890 for tetanus, in 1896 for typhoid fever and in 1897 for bubonic plague, also known as the Black Death. That disease had been the scourge of Europe, with regular plagues killing huge chunks of the population. It took a vaccine to finally

bring it down. It still hangs on in some remote corners of the world, where wild animals still carry it, but thanks to modern medicine it will never be the horror that it once was.

In the twentieth century, new vaccines came thick and fast: for tuberculosis, or TB (in Ireland, TB killed at least 10,000 people every year), for diphtheria, scarlet fever, yellow fever, influenza, polio, measles, mumps, rubella, meningitis and hepatitis B. One by one, diseases that killed millions were beaten back, controlled, eliminated. In 1980, it was declared that smallpox was officially eradicated around the globe. Please, a *bualadh bos* for vaccines!

IMMUNE ACTIVATION

But how exactly do vaccines work against infectious organisms? The fact that cowpox could be used as a preventive against smallpox gave us a big clue. We now know that the cowpox virus is similar to the smallpox virus, and yet it doesn't cause that disease. The similarity means that when the body is injected with cowpox, it sets off an immune response which clears the mild infection. When someone is then infected with smallpox, the immune system has been trained by its exposure to cowpox to kill the smallpox, because it recognises the parts of smallpox that are similar to cowpox. If the body hasn't seen cowpox, smallpox will run wild, causing serious disease.

It's a bit like a party where, let's say, rowdy fans of a football team wearing their team colours try to get in (cowpox). A security man stops them. More fans then turn up, wearing the same colours as the previous fans, but this time perhaps carrying weapons (smallpox). The security man recognises the team colours and says, 'Not tonight, lads.'

Vaccines today are mainly of two types: dead or inactivated organisms (weakened football fans wearing their team's shirt), or purified parts (the shirt alone). Louis Pasteur was the scientist who came up with the method of inactivation. He was studying chicken cholera, an infectious disease in – you guessed it – chickens. In one experiment, he infected chickens with a batch of cholera mixed into a broth that had been left out and had spoiled. When he then tried to infect the chickens with fresh cholera, he noticed that they were protected. From Blossom's hide to poor chickens having to drink gone-off cholera soup, the history of medicine has a lot to thank animals for. The cholera virus that had gone off had been weakened in some way and no longer caused disease. But it had enough in common with the regular virus to train the immune system to fight it off.

The first vaccines were similar to the chicken cholera that had spoiled. They were inactivated by chemicals or heat (imagine those football fans after a day in the hot sun). These include vaccines against polio, hepatitis A, rabies, yellow fever, measles, mumps, rubella, influenza and typhoid. A lot of different vaccines use the football shirt – purified parts from the infectious agent. This can include vaccines against tetanus and cholera, hepatitis B, influenza and human papilloma virus (HPV).

The study of new vaccines is still ongoing. Influenza, or the flu, is a major focus, as it is very dangerous to vulnerable people like the old, the sick and the very young. There are different types of influenza and the virus can change from season to season, so each flu season might have a different vaccine. Lots of effort is going into the search for vaccines for diseases like malaria and AIDS. These are difficult to vaccinate against because they are caused by very complex processes. One of the most recent vaccine successes has been against the Ebola virus, which is present in parts of West Africa and which causes a highly lethal disease. A major effort to develop a vaccine began following outbreaks in 2013. A vaccine against Ebola was developed in 2015, and new ones are still in development.

The COVID-19 pandemic led to an unprecedented (never seen before) effort to find a vaccine. Every possible strategy was tested: dead virus, live weakened virus and also components (parts) from the virus. The components include the protein in the spikes of the virus, which it uses to get into lung cells. All proteins are made from a genetic recipe. Ribonucleic acid, or RNA, helps to turn the instructions in your DNA into proteins in your cells. The RNA that encodes the spike protein on the virus was tested. If it is injected into your arm muscle, your body makes the spike protein and your immune system can then make antibodies that will bind to the spike protein on the virus if it infects you – like Blu-Tack, it bungs it up and stops the virus entering cells. These antibodies protect you against the virus. The RNA COVID vaccines were carefully tested to make sure they were safe and effective. They were launched in late 2020, a remarkable achievement. They have saved millions of lives.

Herd immunity is another factor in making vaccines effective. This phrase, again, comes from treating cows. If a lot of people are vaccinated, the disease will have nowhere to hide. If you don't get the jab, you are putting other people at risk – people who have a weakened immune system because they are on immunosuppressant drugs (given to people who have had organ transplants or are being treated for an inflammatory disease) or because they have diabetes or heart disease or simply because they are an older person. COVID-19 is especially severe in older people and people with these underlying conditions, making vaccination and herd immunity all the more important to protect the vulnerable.

A TOXIC MIX?

Using vaccines sounds like a no-brainer, right? Bring on the jabs! Well, it's not so simple. Many people worry that vaccines could be dangerous, and these worries have been growing over the past few years. Many people are choosing not to be vaccinated, which can have negative effects on others. Why is there all this worry, and – most important – is there any reason for it?

As we have learned, the main part of a vaccine is made up of either the weakened organism or parts taken from it. Another important part is called the adjuvant. This is a chemical that can boost the immune response, and most vaccines don't work without it. Adjuvants are like jump leads to get a car engine going, and they have been used since the 1950s. They are often chemicals that have frightening names like aluminium hydroxide or monophosphoryl lipid A. The use of these adjuvants or other additives has added to concerns that vaccines can be harmful. But they are safe. Vaccines do contain things like aluminium and formaldehyde, but there's much less of these things in them than what you'd pick up from your everyday environment.

Some parents think that children are being given too many vaccines all at once. It's true that children are being given more vaccines than before and sometimes in combination, but overall, because of scientific advances, the amount of material in each vaccine is a lot less than before. So, in fact, the total amount is less. The amount of material in vaccines is trivial when compared with what you are exposed to in the natural world every day.

What about side effects? Studies show that it is very rare for a person to be harmed by a vaccine. Minor side effects are common – a sore arm or a slight fever. There are more serious side effects. One in 4,000 children will have seizures in response to the MMR vaccine. One study of the HPV vaccine found that out of almost 200,000 girls, it caused 24 cases of fainting. Children often become ill soon after vaccination, but in the vast majority of cases this is a coincidence: illness happens, at the same rate, in unvaccinated children.

Overall, billions of vaccine doses have been given to billions of people, and only a very few have reported serious harm. Obviously, any harm caused by a vaccine can be devastating for the affected person, or parents of a child who had a bad reaction. But given the massive benefits to humanity of vaccination, these few negative events are not enough to prevent vaccine use. The Center for Disease Control in the USA says that vaccines have prevented more than 21 million hospitalisations in the USA, and 732,000 childhood deaths. All those children are still alive because of vaccines.

MISSING INFORMATION

You probably have an uncle or second cousin who thinks that vaccines are the root of all evil. That they contain microchips, or cause cancer, or somehow give you better phone reception.[4] Other people might refuse to get vaccinated, 'just in case', or mistrust what doctors tell them. The COVID-19 pandemic has led to an upswing in concern about these medical matters.

Bad science, bad information and people with bad motives have led to much confusion. One doctor tried to link the MMR vaccine to autism, but his research was later shown to be wrong, dishonest

---

4 The best thing to do in this situation might be to delete Facebook from their phones. Go on – they won't know how to reinstall it and will have to ask you for help!

and even made up. The doctor was later struck off the medical register.[5] Many scientists tried to see if there is a link, but lots of studies have shown no link between MMR and autism. This type of bad science isn't new: when the first smallpox vaccines were used, strange happenings were reported in medical journals, like vaccinated children who would make mooing noises and run around on all fours.

When people are frightened or angry, they are more likely to believe untrue things. Misinformation is a huge problem when it comes to medical advice. With the internet, it can spread like wildfire. Somebody can post something online, and thousands of people will share it without knowing where it came from, or if it is even true. Online platforms are trying to reduce this kind of misinformation. Facebook says that groups and pages sharing anti-vaccine misinformation will be removed from its recommendations. YouTube has said it will remove content that spreads misinformation about all approved vaccines.

Other people believe that vaccination is part of an international plot to make people obey the government – to turn them into cattle, just like the early smallpox vaccine reports suggested. The truth is, if it was so easy to get politicians to work together, we might have already done something about problems like war, famine and climate change! The reality is simpler and more complicated. Life is hard, and it often makes no sense. It is sometimes easier to believe

---

5 But he's not out of work: he has reportedly given lectures on a cruise ship called the *Conspira-Sea*, along with a woman who claims to have visited Mars and a man who says that he has died and been reborn three times.

that there are evil people working behind the scenes to control everything, rather than accept that the world is messy and chaotic. Scientists might make mistakes, but mostly, everyone is trying their best.

Unfortunately, the anti-vax movement has led to measles making a comeback, including in Ireland, where cases more than doubled last year. Even the dreaded polio, which we learned about at the beginning of this chapter, has begun to rear its head again. New diseases will continue to appear and spread, and old ones may come roaring back. In the last few years, we have all seen what happens when a disease runs rampant through the population – lockdowns, hospitalisations, the restrictions of our lives and personal freedoms. Developing a vaccination programme helped get the COVID-19 pandemic under control. Just as vaccines have in the past, and just as they will in the future. We are lucky to have this effective weapon against disease.

The writer Roald Dahl described how his seven-year-old daughter caught measles. He wrote that she seemed to be recovering and was sitting up in bed. He began teaching her how to make farm animals from pipe cleaners, and then he noticed she had trouble with her finger movements. One hour later, she was unconscious, and 12 hours later she was dead. This happened a year before the measles vaccine was developed.

I'll let Roald Dahl give you this chapter's bottom line: 'Today a good and safe vaccine is available to every family, and all you have to do is to ask your doctor to administer it.'

CHAPTER 4

WHY DO WE DO THINGS THAT ARE BAD FOR US?

W E HUMANS ARE a curious bunch. We love trying new things. If early humans hadn't been curious about things like fire, or clothes, or indoor plumbing, we might not be here today. Curiosity is why we became so successful as a species on Earth. It's why we become scientists. And our curiosity and inventiveness allow us to use what science discovers to make things that are useful to us, like machines or new medicines. We've become the most successful species on Earth – all by being curious.

But, as the old saying goes, curiosity killed the cat.[1] This curiosity often leads us towards things that aren't good for us. Sometimes we lose control over doing, taking or using these things to the point where it is harmful to us. This seems stupid. Surely, with our great big brains, we should be able to stop doing things that are bad for us. But for some of us, the part of our brain that controls common sense sometimes doesn't seem to work. It's as if these people have an angel and a devil on their shoulders and they listen to the devil and ignore the angel.

This is addiction. It's a complex problem that can affect anyone, anywhere, anytime. Addiction means that you know something is bad for you, but you keep doing it, even if it has negative consequences for you or your family and friends. But why do some people become addicted to things, while others don't? Why are we built this way, and what can we do when something becomes so addictive that it ruins our lives?

---

1 The full saying is: 'Curiosity killed the cat, but satisfaction brought it back.' The first part of the saying warns us against unnecessary investigations, but the second part shows that the risk might be worth it. That's all well and good until you've blown up your house after mixing those innocent-seeming chemicals together.

BAD BEHAVIOUR

There are two main types of addiction – chemical and behavioural. Chemical addiction means that you are addicted to a substance. Behavioural addiction means you are addicted to an activity – things like gambling, gaming, shopping or the internet. These behaviours can be normal and harmless – we can't avoid the internet, for example – but when a person's use is out of control, it can spiral into an addiction.

Our latest addiction is to our smartphones. For most of us, the alarms on our phones wake us up, and then the stream of notifications begins. The apps and social media sites we use feed our need for social contact, information and fun. Smartphones have been shown to light up the reward centres in our brains, a bit like how addictive drugs work. Here are some signs of problematic smartphone usage – have a look at these and see if you have any:

- You regularly have an intense urge to use your smartphone.
- You spend more time on it than you intend.
- You panic when the battery runs down.
- You keep using it even though you know it's having a negative effect on your life (that's a big one when it comes to addiction).

For young people – and some adults! – video games are another big issue. You might spend a few hours a week playing *Minecraft* or *Animal Crossing*, but if the time you spend gaming is taking over your life, you might be looking at an addiction. Here are some of the warning signs to look out for.

- Thinking about gaming all the time or a lot of the time.
- Feeling bad when you can't play.
- Not being able to stop or even play less.
- Not wanting to do other things that you used to like.
- Having problems at school or home because of your gaming.

The good news is that these addictions can be treated. Talking to a therapist or counsellor can help. These people are specially trained to listen and help you work out your problems. Cognitive behavioural therapy (CBT) is a type of therapy that looks at how your thoughts and emotions affect your behaviour. It helps us identify thought patterns that are making us behave in certain ways. It teaches us to think *about* thinking, and if we can change our thoughts, we can change our behaviour. Of course, prevention is better than cure, so it's best to keep an eye on your own habits. Set yourself limits – and stick to them. Your brain will thank you!

CHEMICAL CRAVINGS

The other type of addiction is chemical. This involves drugs that affect our brain and behaviour. Some are legal – like alcohol or prescription drugs – but most are illegal, to protect us from ourselves.

Drugs are nothing new. Mead, an alcoholic drink made from fermented honey, was first used about 8000 BCE, and ancient Irish monks made a form of ale.[2] The ancient Sumerians, Chinese, Egyptians and Europeans all used different types of natural drugs made from plants and herbs. The first modern drug was invented in 1804 by a German scientist. He extracted the main active chemical from opium, which comes from poppies. He named it morphine, after Morpheus, one of the Greek gods of sleep, because – you guessed it – it makes you sleepy. It also worked wonders against pain. During the American Civil War, wounded soldiers were treated with this new-fangled wonder drug. Doctors loved it, as it worked quickly and the patient went away happy. But many soldiers returned from the war addicted – they needed the drug to function and would do anything to get more.

---

2 They got in the habit.

Until 1912, opiate drugs like morphine were actually sold in over-the-counter cough syrups. Doctors could also prescribe heroin, another opiate, for irritable babies (it certainly calmed them down), insomnia and 'nervous conditions'. Then, in 1914, the government recognised how damaging these drugs could be and they were banned. To pass these laws, politicians, the media and even doctors played on racist fears of ethnic minorities using these drugs to cause crime and havoc. This discriminatory stereotype continued throughout the twentieth century, and there is evidence that drug policies still unfairly target minority groups. Later, laws banning drugs were changed to allow doctors to prescribe opiates. Sadly, as a result of over-prescription, America is currently going through a modern opiate crisis, with millions addicted to these dangerous drugs.

Alcohol is probably the most used drug in the world.[3] It is created when yeast changes the natural sugars in fruits or grains into alcohol. Alcohol can be used as a cleaner, as an antiseptic or as a sedative, while many people drink it for enjoyment. But alcohol is poison to our bodies. Luckily, the liver does a great job at breaking it down. The problem is, our livers can only handle one standard drink per hour, so if a person drinks more than that the alcohol starts to cause damage. Long-term binge drinking (drinking a lot of alcohol in a short time) increases the risk of liver disease – the liver eventually becomes so scarred by the repeated injury that it packs

---

3 There's another drug that is so common that it is sold in nearly every shop. Your parents or teacher might even be addicted. A tablespoon of it in its pure form will kill you, but some people feel like death without it. The answer? Caffeine.

up altogether. It also increases the risk of various types of cancer, heart disease and stroke.

Nicotine, found in cigarettes and vaping products, is the next most popular addictive chemical. Nicotine is made from the tobacco plant and has an impact on how the brain works. It can cause an increase in blood pressure, heart rate, flow of blood to the heart and a narrowing of the arteries (vessels that carry blood).

Cannabis is the most used illegal drug in Ireland, followed by MDMA and cocaine. Other serious drugs include amphetamines and heroin. People can also become addicted to prescription drugs. All these drugs are dangerous, but especially for young people whose brains are still developing. Drugs have a much more intense effect on younger brains, can slow brain development, and can also lead to mental health disorders including depression, personality disorders and even psychosis (losing touch with reality).

Each country has different laws about controlling drugs. Some people think any damaging substance should be completely banned. Some say that if drugs were available legally, they could be regulated and taxed, and the fact that drugs are illegal leads to crime. Others say that it should come down to personal freedom. However, until we can fully understand how to avoid the damage that addiction does, it's unlikely that most drugs will be legalised anytime soon.

In 1919, the USA banned the sale, manufacture and transportation of alcohol. But these laws failed spectacularly – after the ban, criminal gangs gained control of the beer and liquor supply in many cities, and crime skyrocketed. The laws were repealed in 1933 and alcohol became legal again. This shows us that banning something and pretending it doesn't exist doesn't usually work. If we want to reduce the terrible effects of addiction, it's better for everyone to have all the facts.

FRANTIC ABOUT FOOD

Whatever about illegal drugs that are bad for us, there's one thing we can't ban: food. We need it to survive, and we also like it – a lot. But we live in Stone Age bodies that evolved for conditions 200,000 years ago. Back then, food was scarce – there was no such thing as a takeaway, or even a shop – so when we got food, we ate as much of it as we could. When we were full, any extra was stored in our body as fat. The energy released when we burn fat is huge, and so our bodies store fat away for a rainy day when we're starving. The problem is that we're getting too many sunny days and

not enough rainy days. On top of this, our primitive ancestors had a lifestyle where they hunted, caught an animal, ate it and then ran on. Nowadays, we spend a lot more time sitting still, which means we don't use as much energy and our bodies store the excess food as fat.

And then there's the food itself. Our bodies evolved to eat fruit, vegetables, nuts and some meat – not processed foods filled with fat and sugar.[4] High-sugar and high-fat foods are linked to brain chemicals that give us feelings of pleasure. Not only do they taste delicious and make our brains happy, but highly processed foods might be as addictive as tobacco. Some people are more attracted to fat and sugar, and that seems to be down to the hormones that their bodies produce. Others are more genetically at risk of storing excess fat. This is dangerous because having too much fat is linked to a much higher risk of developing a large number of diseases. These include coronary artery disease, type 2 diabetes, high blood pressure, osteoarthritis, stroke, depression and at least ten cancers, including breast and colon cancer. A combination of our

---

4 Researchers have found that at least some of our cave people ancestors were cannibals, which is not yet recommended as part of a balanced diet. Although, as scientists, we must always keep an open mind.

modern lifestyles and possible genetic factors is leaving us at risk of all these diseases.

Keeping our food intake under control can be tricky. Every so often fad diets come along that promise to shed the pounds. Most are plain nonsense, like eating half a grapefruit with every meal, or drinking three bowls of cabbage soup a day. Aside from making you fart a lot, there's no scientific evidence that these diets work. And worrying too much about our bodies can be incredibly damaging to our mental health. Young people in particular can sometimes develop behaviours and attitudes that are harmful and can have lifelong effects on their bodies. Social media is only making things worse; as humans we naturally tend to compare ourselves to others, even if what we see online isn't real in the first place. The outcome of all of this is serious. It is partly responsible for the epidemic of anxiety, depression and eating disorders in teenagers.

We can't escape food (and we shouldn't want to!), so what's the solution? Keep it simple, stupid – we should all aim to eat nutritious foods and move a little bit more, while remembering that our worth is not connected to our appearance. We're always on the hunt for a quick fix, but the tortoise will always win over the hare. Making small changes means we're much more likely to stick to them. If we go easy on the junk food, keep our bodies moving, and mind our own minds, we'll stay on the right track.

FINDING THE CAUSE

With this long, long list of chemicals or behaviours that lead to addiction, you would imagine that everyone should be addicted to something. But that's not the case, which brings up the next question: Why do some of us escape addiction and others don't?

As with other human traits, the answer will lie somewhere between nature (your genetic background) and nurture (the environment you grow up in). This is because addiction comes from a combination of environment and genetics – it will be driven by our nature *through* how we are nurtured. People may well have certain genetic variants that put them at risk, but that will only be revealed if the person is in a particular environment. Understanding more about this is important to help people who desperately want to escape their addiction.

There is no doubt that genetic factors play an important role, but even those at a low genetic risk who are exposed to high doses of an addictive substance over a period of time will become addicted. For many drugs, it seems to be a matter of dosage. There's a well-known statement in medicine: everything we consume is a poison, it's just a matter of dose. Case in point: chocolate. Even if you are Bruce Bogtrotter from *Matilda,* eating too much of it can kill you. For a human, it's about 40 kg of milk chocolate. For a dog, it's much lower – even a small amount can be lethal.

Studies suggest that around half of a person's risk of becoming addicted is based on his or her genetic makeup. It looks like some of us have a lower threshold for addiction than others. This might

be caused by genetic differences – a sensitivity in the brain causes pathways that lead to addiction being triggered. Environmental factors are just as important. If we know the environmental factors, there's a chance we might be able to intervene and change them to reduce the risk. A number of influences have been studied: lack of parental supervision, pressure from peers, drug availability and poverty are all risk factors. Difficult childhood experiences are strongly associated with the risk of addiction later in life. The quality of the nurturing (caring) a child gets in early childhood is especially important.

And then there's advertising, that sneaky hand on our shoulder, directing us towards things we know are bad for us. You won't see billboards advertising illegal drugs, but ads for alcohol, gambling and junk food still pop up regularly. Since 2009, it has been illegal to advertise tobacco in Ireland, and alcohol can only be advertised at certain times of the day. But studies in the USA show that children under the age of seven who see a lot of advertisements for fast food or sugary drinks develop a habit for these foodstuffs that becomes hard to break.

A MODERATE MONKEY

The phrase 'to have a monkey on your back' means that you have a problem you can't get rid of.[5] Often that problem is a substance or behaviour that is having a negative effect on your life. It's important

---

5 Monkeys can also suffer from addiction. Vervet monkeys living on the Caribbean island of St Kitts have developed a taste for alcohol and some even steal cocktails from tourists.

to realise that whatever your genetics or your upbringing, nobody is destined to be an addict. Certain factors might make you more likely to behave in ways that are bad for you, but that is never the end of the story.

The first step to recovery is the toughest: the person must recognise they have a problem and decide to make a change. Recovery usually starts with talking to a doctor, who will know how to help. Then the person will have to make behavioural changes and avoid triggers. Counselling will help the addict identify the root causes of their addiction, repair relationships and learn coping skills. It's important for people to know that being addicted to drugs or a behaviour is not a character flaw or a sign of weakness: it is due to a combination of factors. There is always hope. The monkey of addiction might cling on for dear life, but with the right help, a person can break free completely. If you or a family member or friend are suffering from addiction, there is help out there. The first step is asking for it.

Doing things in moderation is very old-fashioned these days. We binge-watch entire series, eat whole pizzas, and watch a zillion online videos in one session. Everything is either the worst or the best, people are either good or evil – there's no room for the middle ground. We evolved to see things in black and white, rather than shades of grey. If you have to make life-or-death decisions in a split second, this can be useful – that tiger will *definitely* eat me if I don't run away, or I should eat *all* those tasty berries in case I don't find any tomorrow. The problem is that we aren't living in that kind of world any more. Moderation might not sound like much fun, but the science backs it up – doing something too much and too often lessens the pleasure.

The bottom line: We all do things that are bad for us from time to time. If we fall into an addiction, this can be treated. And if you want to really enjoy anything – whether it's a new video game or that extra cheesy pizza – take it one bite at a time.

CHAPTER 5

WHY
DO WE
BREAK
THE
LAW?

I N APRIL 2019, I was invited to Mountjoy Prison in Dublin, one of Ireland's largest prisons, to give a talk to some prisoners who had read and enjoyed my book *Humanology*. The day before I was due to go in, the teacher who had invited me reminded me not to bring my mobile phone or laptop as they would be kept by security on the way in. She wrote: *Hope you're not scared coming in to visit us!* I emailed back: *I am now!*

I spent three hours in the jail, talking to around a hundred prisoners about the origin of life, how humans evolved, what makes us human and where we might be going as a species. I told them that the Earth is 4.5 billion years old and said that this is a very long time. A prisoner shouted out: 'Not as long as three years in here!' I had a tremendous time, was heckled constantly, and got a tiny sense of what it's like to be in prison.

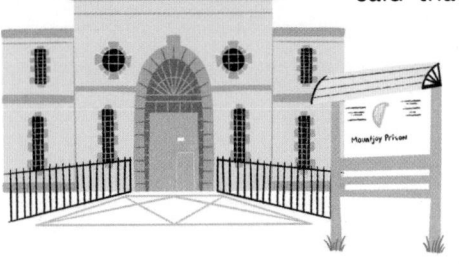

On my way out, I asked the teacher what the men who had come to my talk were in jail for. She didn't tell me, but she did say something interesting. She said some of them had committed serious crimes, but that almost all of them were 'just like you'. This struck a chord. Why was it me standing up there giving a talk to them about my book, as opposed to one of them standing in front of me, sitting there as a prisoner? Why do some of us commit crimes and some of us do not? Why do we have laws in the first place? And what do we do when someone breaks the law?

LAWFUL LIVING

The idea of laws probably began thousands of years ago, when tribes started to get bigger and rules were needed to keep us on our best behaviour. If you did something bad, like steal from your neighbour, it would threaten the safety of the entire tribe. This care for each other also made sure that the copies of our DNA in our relatives would get passed on. It is possible that crime becomes a feature of society when it reaches a certain number of people. Think of society like a classroom with a substitute teacher: the bigger the class, the rowdier it gets, until all the windows are broken and the poor teacher is in tears. Smart people in the tribe – the elders, or parents – would have come up with ways to make members behave, since there is a natural tendency for people to stray from the path and become what in Ireland are called 'messers'.

One way to convince people to behave is to tell them that some kind of supernatural being is watching over them. This may have been the start of religion – obey the rules, or god will punish you. All religions describe sin, which is a crime against the laws set down by whichever god you believe in. The Old Testament dates back to 1280 BCE and is full of laws, the most important being the Ten Commandments, which covered the main crimes at that time. The Jewish Torah contains 613 laws, although some of them are no longer used, while Sharia, Islam's legal system, comes from the holy book of the Quran. Another well-known list is the seven deadly sins: pride, greed, lust, envy, gluttony, wrath and sloth. Any one of these might make you commit a crime, although I'm not quite sure how sloth fits in – surely you are too lazy to do much? Maybe you're too lazy to pay your taxes, which is a crime.

Some countries have laws built on religious beliefs. Some Middle Eastern countries, like Saudi Arabia, have laws based on Islamic teachings. Until 2018, abortion was illegal in Ireland because it went against Catholic teaching. Other countries, like the USA, try to avoid this – the first item on the Bill of Rights, which is an addition to the American Constitution, says, 'Congress shall make no law respecting an establishment of religion.' It is debatable whether this has been successful.

Wherever laws come from, they have the same goal: to make sure people behave themselves in society. If they step out of line and break the law, they must be punished. Every country has a constitution of some sort that sets out the laws of the state. Governments can suggest new laws which are then voted on, either by politicians or the people themselves. There are different types of laws, including laws against violent offences, sexual offences, offences against property, offences against the state, use of illegal drugs, and financial offences. Some crimes involve actual harm to others (such as assault), while others are about decreasing the risk of harming others (such as traffic offences). Laws are constantly changing and being updated. Once cars were invented, for example, a whole set of laws were needed to regulate behaviour, like speed limits and wearing seatbelts. Once the internet became widespread, we needed laws about online harassment and stealing digital property. Other laws become obsolete as society moves on – in Arizona, it is illegal to allow your donkey to sleep in your bathtub (although it's probably better to keep this one on the books).

The fact that we needed to invent laws in the first place tells us that we are prone to misbehaving. In a perfect world, everyone would be on their best behaviour all the time, singing songs about rainbows and friendship. Obviously, that's not the case – so are we hardwired to break the rules?

CRIMINAL GENE-IUS

As long as there have been laws, there have been law-breakers. The first scientific attempt to explain why some people commit crimes was in 1876, when Cesare Lombroso, an Italian criminologist, came up with the theory of 'anthropological determinism'.[1] Lombroso said that there were 'born criminals' who you could spot from their physical features. According to Lombroso, these included large jaws, low and sloping foreheads, handle-shaped ears, a hawk-like nose and long arms – and that was just the men. Lombroso also studied female criminals. He said that they showed fewer signs of 'degeneration' because they had 'evolved less than men due to the inactive nature of their lives'. He thought that women weren't intelligent enough to be criminals. It might be tempting to prove Lombroso wrong, but please don't – you'll get me in trouble.

---

1 It should be a crime to come up with long words to boast about how smart you are. I would never do that because I suffer from sesquipedalophobia.

Obviously, Lombroso was way off, but lots of sociologists, psychologists and neuroscientists have since tried to work out why some people commit crimes and others don't. Sadly, the science behind their conclusions is often wrong or badly presented. There can also be bias (as we can see from Lombroso, who clearly didn't like women) and racism (suggesting that certain ethnic groups are more likely to commit crimes). The experts do agree on one thing: the reason why someone commits a crime is rarely down to one thing; it is usually caused by a lot of factors, making it difficult to unravel.

The statistics of who is in prison for what crime can be revealing. Prisoners are more likely to come from a deprived area than a rich one. Some cannot read or write. Most people in prison in Ireland have never sat a state examination, and over 50 per cent left school before the age of 15. A lot more men are in prison than women, and crimes committed by men are much more likely to be serious or violent. There may be several reasons for this, including social or cultural factors, crimes not being reported, and biological factors, such as higher testosterone, which might lead to aggression.

The first clue as to why men commit more crimes than women begins in childhood. Boys are much more likely to break the law at a young age than girls. Studies have shown that girls are less likely than boys to have learning difficulties and behavioural problems in childhood. These early difficulties may set boys on a different life course when compared with girls. Among young men, fewer opportunities lead to men working in low-paid jobs and, as a result, they may be tempted by crime. Several studies have shown that as the rate of unemployment increases, so does the crime rate.

Testosterone, a hormone that is produced in higher amounts in men, may play a part in making men more aggressive. Testosterone drives males to be more competitive, find more resources and seek a mate. This, in turn, can lead to crime, including theft and violence. Research has shown that testosterone levels in prisoners were highest in the most violent criminals, and they also broke more rules in prison, especially rules involving confrontation. Many studies show that men are much more likely to be verbally or physically aggressive. Interestingly, men are much more likely than women to engage in cyberbullying (bullying that takes place online, especially on social media). But as well as committing crimes, men are also much more likely to be victims of crime.

We're still left with the question of why one person, male or female, will commit a crime and another will not. As with most complex traits in humans, the answer will lie somewhere between nature and nurture – what traits we are born with and how we are raised.

In terms of how a person is raised, several things stand out. Fear of punishment or rejection keeps most of us from behaving badly. During childhood, most people take on board society's rules and they feel guilt, shame and low self-esteem if they break a rule. But some people don't feel this way – this is known as antisocial behaviour. This can happen because of peer pressure, which teenagers are prone to. Witnessing violence as a child can also have a damaging effect. A key risk factor is a broken or unstable family life, which can mean neglect, poor communication, pent-up emotions or, at its worst, physical or sexual abuse. Someone who has been rejected by their family can find a sense of belonging in a criminal gang.

These are all environmental factors that can lead to criminal behaviour. But what about nature? Can a person be 'born to be bad'? Looking at twins can be very interesting. Identical twins will have the exact same genes, while fraternal twins are like regular siblings. If the crime rate between identical twins is the same as between fraternal twins, then it's likely that environmental factors are important, since twins will grow up in similar environments.[2] But if the crime rate is higher between identical twins, then that would suggest genetics play a bigger role. And, overall, studies of twins support the idea that genetics is an important factor in who will become a criminal. We can also look at children who are adopted. Studies have found that children who had a parent with a criminal record, and who were adopted into non-criminal families, had a higher rate of being a criminal themselves. A person might not be born bad, but these studies show that genetics *are* a factor.

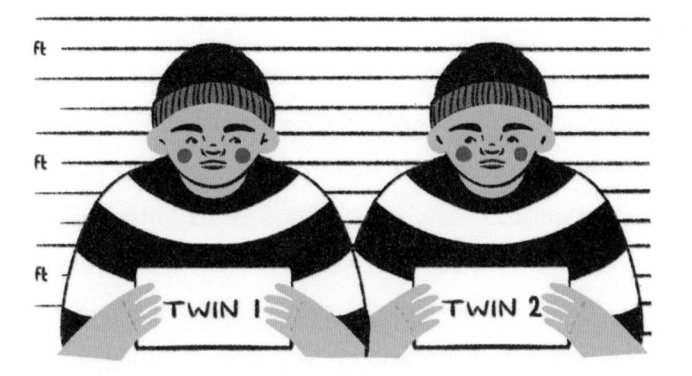

---

2   Unless they are separated at birth and only meet many years later in hilarious circumstances. We've all seen a movie or TV show with this plotline. If this happened as often as Hollywood seems to think it does, it would be very useful to behavioural scientists.

The next question is: What genes give people a higher risk of being a criminal? The strongest evidence has been found in a gene that makes an enzyme called monoamine oxidase-A (or MAO-A, which is much more fun to say). It's the job of MAO-A to control the chemicals in our brains. Studies show that having a less active form of MAO-A makes people more sensitive, more affected by bad experiences, and more defensive and aggressive. Why exactly this happens, we aren't sure, but scientists have looked at animals to try to find clues. Scientists deleted the MAO-A gene in mice, and the mice became highly aggressive, reactive and bitey. Studies in primates have also provided additional evidence that MAO-A levels are important for aggression. Macaque monkeys with genes that produce less MAO-A, who were raised without their mothers, are much more competitive and aggressive. This lines up with what is reported in humans – lower MAO-A levels makes a person mighty bitey and fighty.

Strangely enough, studies have shown that a *more* active version of MAO-A predicts aggressive antisocial behaviour in females. This is difficult to explain, as less active MAO-A leads to aggressive behaviour in males. This might be due to what are called modifiers: things that change the effect of a gene. Testosterone could be a modifier. Men have higher levels of testosterone, and maybe more testosterone means more aggression if the men have lower MAO-A. If there is less testosterone, as in females, perhaps high levels of MAO-A become problematic.

It's tempting to throw our hands up at this stage and say: who knows! But that's the thing about science. It might be tempting to say that somebody can be born bad, or taught to be bad, or even bad because they have a lumpy head and big ears. But an easy answer is rarely a right answer, and this is too important to get wrong. Many people love the idea of superheroes – a good guy versus a bad guy. The good guy uses his (or her) laser eyes, or super strength, or magic hammer, to catch the bad guy, who is usually threatening to rob a granny or blow up the moon. But the reality is that life isn't that simple. Nobody is born a bad guy, just as nobody is born with superpowers.

I am still left with the question – why is it that I wasn't a prisoner in Mountjoy listening to someone else give a lecture? The answer is probably that I had a loving and stable upbringing, didn't suffer any hardships as a child, had a peer group who didn't have any criminal tendencies (probably thanks to my mother, who made sure I went to a good school and who always kept an eye on my friends) and last, in all likelihood had a genetic makeup that didn't nudge me towards becoming a criminal if I had lived in more difficult circumstances. In other words, I was lucky.

What can we do to help others who are not so lucky, either to decrease the chances of them becoming criminals or to try to be sure that they won't re-offend? We have to support those in need of help and try to reduce the emotional pain that might lead to criminal behaviour. It has to start with our children. Experts suggest that we need to treat violent behaviour as a public health concern, using technology to reach every child so that they all feel cared for. Proactive community and school programmes must be supported and encouraged. Family and community support are essential. Governments have to look beyond law enforcement and criminal justice.

One thing is certain – just throwing people into jail doesn't work. A lot of research finds that spending time in prison doesn't lower the risk that someone will offend again. In some cases, it actually makes it more likely that they will commit crimes after they leave prison. So if we truly want less crime in our societies, we need to be sure we are getting this right.

THE COLOUR OF JUSTICE

One thing it is important to remember is that laws don't always define what is right and wrong. The legal system can be used to oppress, control and unfairly punish. In the USA, for much of the twentieth century, segregation laws meant that black and white people weren't allowed to mix. Until recently, women were not allowed to drive in Saudi Arabia, and homosexuality is illegal in many countries around the world. Many governments throw their political opponents into jails, pretending that they have broken some law. In the USA, there are 2 million people in prisons, which is a 500 per cent increase over the last 40 years. Changes in sentencing law, not changes in crime rates, explain most of this

increase. Many of those imprisoned are from racial minorities. Laws also frequently change – what was illegal yesterday may not be illegal today, and vice versa.

Who gets to decide what laws are fair? How do we make sure people are treated equally under the law? There's no easy answer to these big questions, but it's good to keep them in mind when considering how the legal system works.

Here's another one: How do we know the difference between right and wrong in the first place? Current evidence suggests that we are all born with an innate sense of morality, which parents and society can help develop. Scientists studied five-month-old babies to see if they knew the difference between good and bad behaviour. They began with a puppet show. In the show, a cat is seen trying to open a plastic box. A rabbit then appears in a green T-shirt and helps the cat open the box. The scene is repeated, but then a rabbit comes along in an orange T-shirt, closes the box and runs off. The green rabbit is helpful, and the orange rabbit is mean. The baby is then presented with the two rabbits from the show. Just under three-quarters of the babies prefer the 'good' rabbit. It seems that we know right from wrong when we see it, but it's probably not as easy as looking at the colour of a person's T-shirt.

The bottom line: There's one golden rule that all religions and ethical traditions share: treat others kindly and fairly and expect kindness and fairness in return. You don't have to be a prophet to aim for that.

CHAPTER 6

WHY DO WE BELIEVE IN THINGS WE CAN'T SEE?

O NCE UPON A time, the fairy folk put a curse on a road in County Clare. This wasn't in the distant past – it was 1999, and the motorway was being built as part of a plan to bypass Newmarket-on-Fergus and Ennis. But a local storyteller warned that a fairy bush lay in the path of the proposed road. If it was destroyed, he said, it could cause bad luck for people travelling the road. He said the bush was a marker in a fairy path and it was the meeting point for Kerry fairies on their way to do battle with the Connacht fairies. The motorway plans were tweaked and the fairy bush was left where it was.

For thousands of years, humans have believed in supernatural beings – like fairies – that influence our lives. Greek myths and legends are full of monsters, giants and other fantastic creatures. In ancient Egypt, mythological creatures had exciting names like Ammit, Devourer of the Dead; Bennu, the Bird of Fire; El Naddaha, the Siren of the Nile; and Apep, the Enemy of Light. During the Middle Ages in Europe, a lot of people believed in witches, and they became very unpopular – many were accused of wicked, wicked behaviour like souring milk and being argumentative. Even some famous scientists believed in the supernatural – Carl Linnaeus, who classified many species of animals and plants in the eighteenth century, also included magical creatures like the hydra and believed in mermaids.

We might think that nowadays, in the age of flatscreen TVs and electric cars, these beliefs have died out. But most of the people in the world still believe in a supernatural god figure or have spiritual beliefs. One 2019 poll found that nearly 50 per cent of Americans believe that demons and ghosts either 'probably exist' or 'definitely exist'. Where do these beliefs come from? Why do we believe in things we can't see? Can we trust our eyes in the first place? What does the science tell us?

GOD, GOBLINS AND GHOSTS

Back when humans lived in small tribes, knowledge and wisdom were passed down from generation to generation. This advice probably helped us survive in a dangerous world: work hard, don't hurt people, look after your family. These rules meant that the DNA belonging to you and your relatives would get passed on. The elders of the tribe would have come up with ways to make members follow this advice, as we read about in the chapter on breaking the law. Appealing to a supernatural being in the sky was very effective. And where there's light, there's dark – the idea of a loving god and a hostile devil is common in many religions. When someone did something wrong, evil beings like demons and fairies and mischievous spirits were often blamed.

Why religion has survived in our modern world is an interesting question. One answer is that following those same rules – work hard, don't hurt people, look after your family – benefits society as a whole. Another is that many studies show that religious people are healthier than non-believers and tend to get along well with others, work hard, be punctual, and are able to control impulsive behaviours. Religions often focus on looking out for each other and on social activities (such as religious ceremonies or fundraisers), and we know that social activity helps us a lot – it decreases the risk of heart disease, for example.

Myths and legends likely come from the same place as religion and have survived for similar reasons. Imagine a child who is starting to explore the world outside their village. But their anxious father says, 'Don't go into the forest, there's a bogeyman in there.' And the child will believe him. They won't seek evidence for the bogeyman, because their brain is set up to receive and believe the information. They will find it very hard to escape this belief in the bogeyman and might even carry it with them for the rest of their life. Fairy tales also have the same purpose. Little Red Riding Hood teaches us to avoid the dark woods, because they are full of big bad wolves with a taste for old women.[1]

---

1 In the original version, a woodcutter comes to the rescue with an axe and cuts open the sleeping wolf's stomach to let Little Red Riding Hood and her grandmother escape. Then they fill the wolf's body with heavy stones and it dies. While wolves can be forgiven for acting like wolves, it takes humans to come up with something this nasty.

People also came up with stories to help explain natural things that happened around them. Thunderstorms were caused by an angry sky god. Floods were the work of a river god. When someone got sick or injured themselves, it was easier to believe that a witch had cast a spell on them rather than accepting that life can be random and chaotic. This kind of magical thinking is common in children and is a natural part of a child's development. A monster lives under the bed, and the only thing that can make it disappear is a special monster spray. But as we grow, we learn about cause and effect and logic replaces magical thinking.

Supernatural beliefs can also be comforting when we have to deal with the loss of loved ones. We want to remain connected to them in some way, even after death. A ghost is believed to be a manifestation of the spirit or soul of a person. If you believe in ghosts, you're not alone. Cultures all around the world believe in spirits that survive death to live in another world. Some people report ghostly encounters that are helpful, such as a loved one giving them advice. Others are more sinister – hauntings of the sort we might see in a horror movie. Hauntings have been reported to include strange sounds, flashing lights, cold temperatures or coded messages.

Some paranormal experiences are easily explainable, based on faulty activity in the brain or outside factors like electrical problems. Orbs of light or strange shapes that show up in photos are often particles of dust or moisture. Many ghost sightings happen at night and might be caused by sleep paralysis. This is when our bodies are paralysed – which happens every night when we sleep – but our brains are still partly awake. This often brings a feeling of dread and hallucinations (seeing something that isn't there) of anything from spiders to ghosts. A lot of paranormal experiences come down to something called 'priming' – if we are primed to see something spooky, we are more likely to see something spooky. Many supernatural events are simply hoaxes. So when it comes to ghosts, we have to turn to the philosophical theory called Occam's razor, which says that the simplest solution is usually the correct one. No hard scientific proof has ever backed up the existence of the paranormal. For now, ghosts are definitively busted.

But that's not to say that supernatural beliefs and superstitions are useless. One study has found that superstitions can boost performance in a range of skills. In one trial, subjects did better on a memory test if they brought their favourite lucky charm with them, since it seemed to increase their confidence. Another experiment tested the subjects' golfing ability. Telling them that they were using a 'lucky' ball meant they were more likely to score than those simply using any old ball. Even something as simple as saying 'break a leg' or 'I'll keep my fingers crossed for you' improved their performances.

All this invention and imagination might seem like a lot of effort. But we love stories like this because they help us develop our brains. Brain scans have shown that reading or hearing stories activates areas of the cortex that are known to be involved in social and emotional processing, and the more people read fiction, the easier they find it to empathise with other people. The safe, imaginary world of a story may be a kind of training ground where we can practise interacting with others and learn the customs and rules of society. And stories are good at persuading and motivating us because they appeal to our emotions. So inventing all sorts of gods, goblins and ghosts has had an evolutionary benefit. And when you remember that for most of human history, people have lived in the dark – no candles, no lamps, no electric lights – it's easy to understand how we came to believe in invisible things that go bump in the night.

TRICK OF THE EYE

When it comes to things we can't see, it's not just the supernatural that we believe in. We believe that two magnets will stick together, despite not seeing the magnetism. We believe that our phones will connect to the internet, even if we can't see the Wi-Fi. Unlike many animals, we can't see ultraviolet light. Other species, like snails, frogs and lobsters, can detect Earth's magnetic field, and some birds rely on it for navigation. Czech and German scientists have even concluded that dogs poo in alignment with the Earth's magnetic field. They studied 37 breeds of dog over two years, with a total of 1,893 poos and 5,582 wees, recording the orientation of the dog with a compass. Yes, weely! It's obvious that what our eyes tell us isn't the whole story.

And we can't always trust what we see. The human brain is an incredibly complex organ with the ability to create something out of nothing. Hallucinations are where you hear, see, smell, taste or feel things that appear to be real but only exist in your mind. Drugs, mental disorders and certain types of illness can all produce this effect – someone might hear voices or see a person who isn't there.

Our brains are also very easy to fool. An optical illusion is a trick that our minds play based on contextual clues. It can make us see things that aren't there, make a pattern out of seemingly unrelated objects, or switch our perspective. One of the most famous of these is the rabbit/duck illusion. If you haven't seen it, it is an image of a rabbit with long ears, but if you tilt your head a certain way it becomes a duck with a beak. Two people could look at the exact same picture and see two completely different animals.

Another interesting phenomenon is pareidolia: this is seeing images, like a human face, an animal or an object, in random patterns. Studies have found that people who believe in the supernatural are more likely to see hidden faces in everyday photos. Often, people show up in the news claiming that Jesus Christ has appeared on a slice of their toast, or Elvis Presley's face is visible in the knots on their doors, or they've captured a ghost in the background of a photo. These are usually examples of pareidolia: seeing a familiar pattern where no pattern exists. Another example is the constellations. We've all grown up knowing how to see certain shapes in the stars, like the Plough or Orion's Belt. Of course, these don't actually exist – humans just draw lines with their minds to link up the distant stars into shapes we can make sense of. After all, it takes real imagination to see a lion in the Leo constellation or a flying horse in Pegasus![2]

The reason for this is thought to be evolutionary. Our brains tend to arrange complex images or designs into an organised system, something that we can easily recognise. Part of this process is taking an image and then quickly sifting through our catalogue of all

---

2 Constellations vary from culture to culture. The Plough is the Big Dipper in America and the Great Bear in Germany. The Aboriginal people of Australia have their own constellations, including the Dark Emu, which can be seen in the Milky Way. Its position in the sky tells them whether they should be out hunting for emus or collecting their eggs.

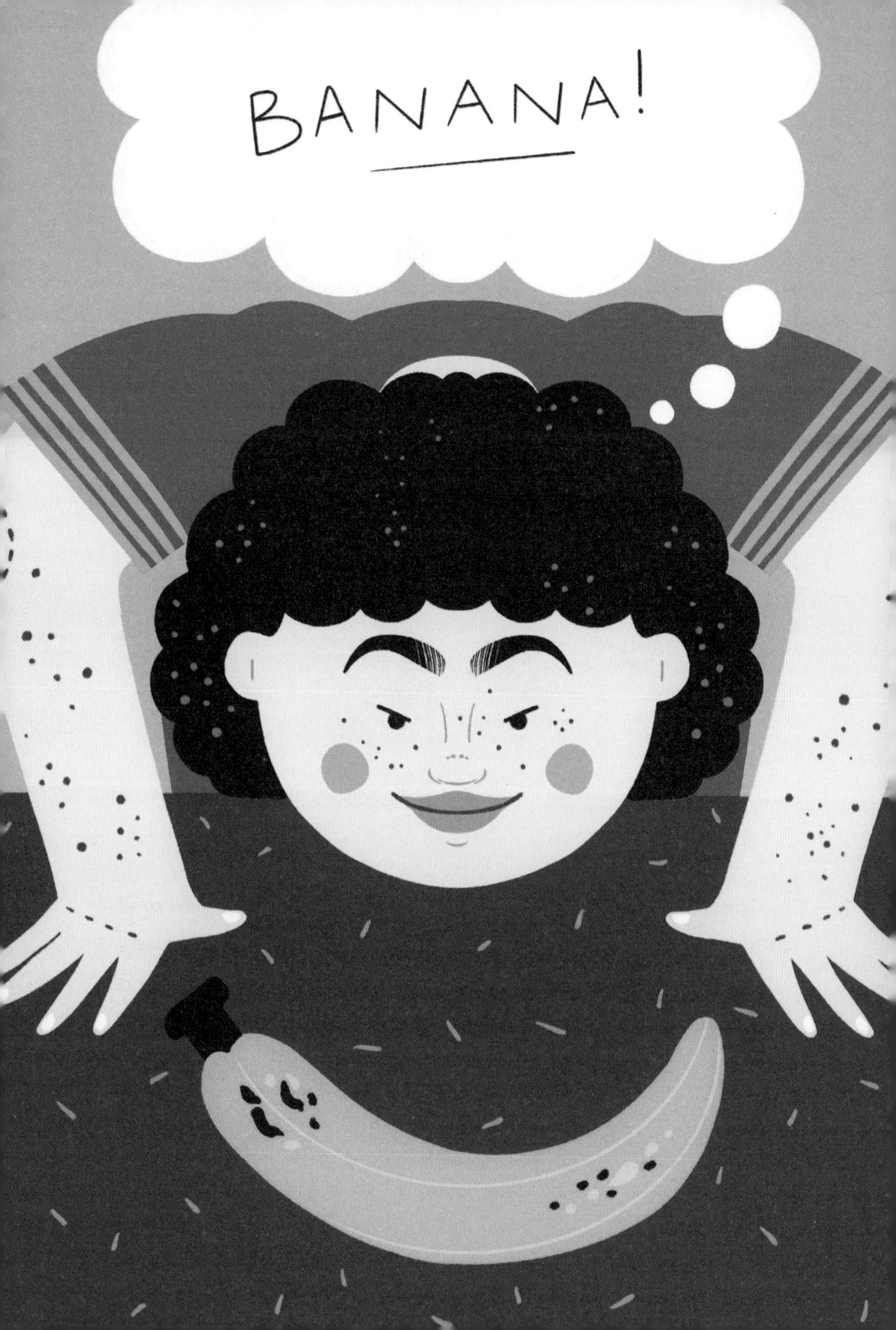
BANANA!

possible matches, finding the best match, and then assigning it to the image. That cloud looks like a horse, so your brain matches it to a horse and then fills in more details to make it look even more like a horse.

We are particularly likely to see faces. Studies have shown that the brain lights up when it sees a facial pattern. A part of our visual cortex, the fusiform face area, specialises in recognising and remembering faces. Even young babies will spend more time looking at a human face than another image of similar complexity. It's easier and safer for us to see a face or a tiger in a patch of grass so we can react to a possible danger. Even if we're wrong nine times out of ten, that one time pays for all, and gets us home safe.

REALITY BITES

When we see something – a banana, for example – the image we create in our minds is based on input from our eyes (yellow and bendy? Must be a banana). Our other senses chime in (this smells and feels like a banana). This is added to by our memories (I have seen a banana before so this must also be a banana), our cultural experiences (mum said bananas are good for me therefore I will eat this tasty banana and enjoy its banana-y flavour). A fairly complex process for our brains, but for us, it happens as fast as we can think.

But what if the sensory inputs we get from the world around us aren't real at all? What if *nothing* we see is real? What if we're living in something like a very advanced video game? The 1999 film *The Matrix* is based on this idea: the bodies of the main characters are plugged into vats to be used as batteries, while their consciousness walks around in a simulated world, thinking it is real. This theory could explain some of the stranger things we see in the world – these are actually glitches in the computer program.

The idea that we live in a simulation seems like a fun thing to imagine, but it turns out that there is actually some science to it. Physicists have thought about the problem and have come up with some interesting suggestions. It's a little tricky, but the idea goes like this:

1. Imagine there are many civilisations like ours dotted all around the universe.
2. Also imagine that many of these civilisations have developed advanced technology that lets them create computer simulations.
3. These civilisations might decide to run a simulation of a time in their own past, looking back on their ancestors' lives, kind of like a history project.
4. If they do this, there will one day be many more simulated minds than real minds.
5. Therefore, it is statistically unlikely that we are actually one of the few real minds in existence rather than one of the trillions of simulated minds.

That could mean that you're reading this book because your great-great-great-great-grandchild is running a simulation of their ancestor reading a book in the distant past ... see? I told you it was tricky. Depending on your outlook, this might all seem incredibly cool or incredibly terrifying. We'll probably never know which is true. Unless our descendants decide to switch off the simula—

The bottom line: Believing in things we can't see has always been a human trait. It gives us evolutionary advantages and is a way to bond with other people. And anyway, reality is what we make of it.

FEMALE BRAIN

MALE BRAIN

CHAPTER 7

WHAT'S THE DIFFERENCE BETWEEN MEN AND WOMEN?

YOU MIGHT HAVE heard the old saying 'men are from Mars and women are from Venus'. That doesn't mean that men live on a dusty, red planet while women chill out in boiling clouds of sulphuric acid. Instead, it means that they are alien species who will never fully understand each other. Once upon a time, this idea was very popular, but we now know that it is as wrong as the moon being made of cheese. Men and women aren't different species – we're all human, and all humans hang out right here on Planet Earth, where we do silly things like breakdance in nightclubs and write terrible poetry, all to impress the opposite sex.

But is 'opposite' the right word to use? Are the sexes so far apart? What are the scientifically proven differences between men and women? Is there a difference between sex, gender and sexual orientation? What makes somebody straight, gay or something else?

These questions are difficult, and people tend to get extremely worked up about them, with lots of wailing and gnashing of teeth. To add to the confusion, the scientific studies that have been done often show bias. 'What?' I hear you say. 'Scientists can be biased?' I'm afraid they can. But, as with all of the issues in this book, we just need to (wo)man up and do our best to reach conclusions based on the science.

LET'S TALK ABOUT SEX

In the animal kingdom, some species show clear physical differences between the sexes. One of the best examples of this is the mandrill

VENUS

monkey. The males wear a lot of make-up on their faces and behinds (well, it's not quite make-up, as the vivid colours appear naturally). There is also a major difference in size between male and female mandrills – males are three times heavier than females! Mandrills are a bit like pheasants: the male pheasant has exotically coloured feathers, a large flamboyant tail and a droopy bit around its eyes called a wattle, while the female is small and dull.

But there are also oddities in the animal kingdom, like the delightfully named triplewart seadevil. These creatures live 2,000 metres underwater. Females are 30 cm long, while males only reach around 1 cm in size – I suppose it makes sharing a bed easier as there's no competition for the duvet. Even stranger, many species of fish can switch their gender. They usually start off as female, and then switch to male later in life so as to reproduce. All clownfish start off as male but change sex to female if their mating partner dies.[1]

---

1 Which means Marlin, the father from *Finding Nemo*, would have actually been Marlene.

In humans, the differences between males and females start off with our chromosomes. These are thread-like strands in our body's cells that contain hundreds, or even thousands, of genes. Genes are sequences of DNA that contain the recipe for all the proteins that make up you and me. Every cell in the human body contains 23 pairs of chromosomes. The 23rd pair of chromosomes is known as the sex chromosome, because this pair decides if you will be born male or female. Females have two X chromosomes, while males have one X and one Y chromosome.

It might come as a surprise to people when they learn that sperm, the ultimate manly cell, can be male or female. The male sperm carry the Y chromosome, and the female sperm

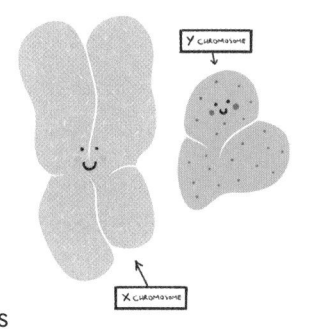

carry the X chromosome. When the male sperm wins the swimming race to get to the egg, the resulting baby will be XY, or male. If the female sperm gets there first, the baby will be XX, or female. What this means is that information present on the Y chromosome will cause male characteristics to develop. The lack of this information will mean that female characteristics will emerge. This differentiation is helped along by hormones produced by either the ovaries or the testes.

What are these characteristics? In our species, males have more hair, deeper voices, more muscle mass, and can produce sperm from testes and a penis. But, of course, some males might have less muscle or body hair, so the idea of a spectrum is important here. Females on average are smaller, with less muscle mass, have higher-pitched voices, can become pregnant and produce milk for their young. Again, all of this exists along a spectrum – it's not a checklist. Some people have a mix of sexual characteristics, which is known as intersex.

So far, so good! Sex chromosomes, helped along by hormones, will produce certain physical characteristics. But once we move away from the physical areas and towards the mental, things get a lot murkier. We will proceed with caution.

THINKING PINK OR BLUE

What are the differences between men and women – apart from physical ones that are plain to see – that scientists agree on? A good way to examine traits in humans is to use a bell curve (because it's shaped like a bell). If we measure the height of lots of men and women and then plot a graph of height versus the frequency of each height (meaning how common each specific height is) in the population, you get a curve. A small number of people will be short and a small number will be tall, and the rest will be in the middle. When we measure height in women and men, we see different curves for each sex. This tells us that men on average are taller than women, although there will be a lot of women who are taller than a lot of men.

We can also use the bell curve to look at non-physical characteristics. If we look at the curve for aggression, we see that on average men are more aggressive than women. This is likely to be due to the hormone testosterone, which is also why men have more

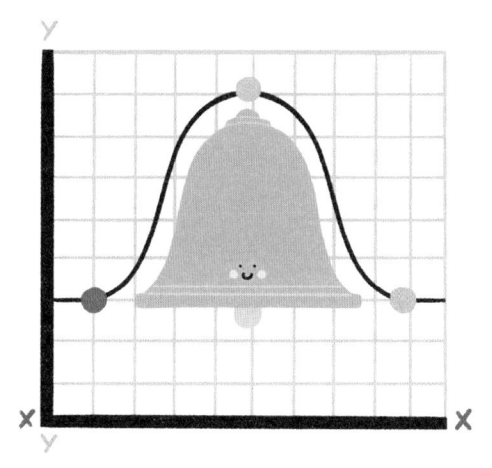

muscle mass than women. But as with all the traits we're talking about, there will be overlap: some women are more aggressive than some men.

Another difference is in health: women suffer more from some diseases, but they still live longer on average than men. In Ireland, life expectancy for women is currently 84 years, while for men it's 80.4 years. The reasons for this difference are not fully understood. Lifestyle differences may be important.

Most scientists agree that men and women perform equally well on IQ tests. Across 4,000 separate studies (which gives you an idea of how exhaustive and exhausting these kinds of studies are), the gap in achievement at maths was largely zero, putting to bed once and for all the notion that men are better at maths. In another study, 31,000 personality tests were analysed (again, a lot in these kinds of studies). The researchers examined many personality traits to see whether these traits were comparable between men and women. They found that women scored higher on anxiety and warmth, while men were more likely to be dutiful and assertive. The other traits showed more minor differences. Of course, the precise reason why women show more warmth but are inclined to have higher levels of anxiety while men are more dutiful and assertive is still unknown. It is likely to be down to a combination of upbringing and a hardwired difference, but how exactly this works is difficult to figure out.

One area where women supposedly shine is empathy, which is defined as the ability to read other people's thoughts and feelings. Surely, I hear you say (what with all your preconceived notions), women will outperform men in that area? Some studies do show that, but if the test is not labelled as an empathy test, any difference goes away, suggesting that it is the tester who shows bias: if they know empathy is being tested, they will grade women higher than men. Another problem with these kinds of studies is how we define warmth or empathy.

Women have been shown to respond differently to someone who is upset or emotional; they are more likely to become upset themselves when they see someone else upset and these feelings will persist. Men, on the other hand, will sense the feelings for a moment and then tune out of the emotion. This tuning out might lead to other parts of the male brain being activated, which are more to do with problem-solving, although this hasn't been proven.

But these tests often come down to filling in questionnaires, which means they are not always that accurate or reliable. People may not answer honestly or may give answers that show themselves in a good light. And just like the scientists performing the tests, the people filling out the surveys will also have their own biases.

Another way to look at difference is to examine male and female brains. The problem is that a lot of nonsense has been published in this area. A study is published claiming a difference, and the media goes wild, with headlines like: YOU WON'T BELIEVE WHAT MEN'S BRAINS ARE MISSING and ARE WOMEN'S BRAINS MADE OF PORRIDGE? ... until other researchers reveal a flaw in the study. It's like a game of whack-a-mole – as soon as one is whacked, another one pops up.

So, are there any physical differences between the male and female brain? Despite a lot of effort, nothing substantial has been found. Female brains are smaller, but this is in proportion to overall body size. In the nineteenth century, when this was noticed, it was known as the 'missing five ounces' – but they were only missing because the overall size of a woman's body is smaller.[2] The differences between men with large heads and men with small heads are as big as the differences between the average man and woman. If you give a neuroanatomist a brain and ask them to say what sex it is, they won't be able to.

A GENDERED WORLD

Without definite physical differences between the male and female brain, the current view is that a gendered world will produce a

---

2   The size of the brain usually increases with the size of the body. Our brains weigh an average of three pounds (1.3 kg), which is enormous for an animal of our body size. The bony-eared assfish has the smallest known brain–body mass ratio of all animals. Yes, that's its real name. Yes, you can use this fact in your next science class.

gendered brain. In other words, the way society treats men and women makes men's and women's brains seem slightly different. Most psychologists agree that differences in personality and emotional intelligence are mainly due to society – they're not hardwired. Babies and children are soaked in pink-versus-blue culture from the moment a parent knows the sex of the foetus. How do we know this culture exists? A study of the most popular television programmes in the USA showed that women mainly have roles that involve relationships – they are friends, family members or romantic partners – whereas men have work-related roles. A study of 5,618 children's books showed that males are represented twice as often as females in book titles and 1.6 times as often as central characters. Men are rarely shown expressing emotions in a positive way, while women are often shown as overly emotional.

This pink/blue culture can also be driven by the environment – a child might observe and copy gendered behaviours they see in the world around them. For males, these behaviours might include assertiveness, ambitiousness and competitiveness; for females they might be more modest behaviour and a focus on relationships. The environment might also involve sex-specific toys and clothes.[3] Children might also be encouraged to act a certain way – little boys are often praised as 'strong', while little girls are told they are 'pretty'. Think about it: has anyone ever described you as a 'brave

---

3 Nowadays, we think of pink for girls and blue for boys. But this hasn't always been the case. A fashion article from 1918 reads: 'The generally accepted rule is pink for the boys, and blue for the girls. The reason is that pink, being a more decided and stronger colour, is more suitable for the boy, while blue, which is more delicate and dainty, is prettier for the girl.'

soldier' or a 'little princess'? These kinds of influences, and many more like them, might go a long way towards explaining why women and men turn out the way they do.

When it comes to occupations, we see big differences between what men and women do. Men are more likely to work with things: they might program computers or repair car engines. Women are more likely to work with people, in professions like medicine or teaching. Again, this could be a result of childhood influences. Why are there so many more male engineers than female? Parental and societal influences are likely to play a role, and one study has shown that women are often discouraged from working with computers. A recent study on gender stereotyping in Ireland also showed something interesting. When children were asked to draw an engineer, 96 per cent of the boys drew a male engineer, while just over 50 per cent of girls drew a female engineer. The study was carried out by students Cormac Harris and Alan O'Sullivan, and the project was the overall winner at the highly competitive 2020 Young Scientists Exhibition.

Another long-running study analysed what schoolchildren draw when they are asked to draw a scientist. Over five decades, 20,860 drawings by students between the ages of five and eight were analysed (yep, that's a lot of drawings). In the 1960s and 1970s, fewer than 1 per cent of the pictures depicted scientists as female; by 2016, that percentage was 34. It was even higher, at 50 per cent, if the drawer was female. This parallels the increase in actual numbers of female scientists in the USA.

Things are definitely getting better in the science world, and elsewhere. A girl in a Western country can expect to be able to do whatever she wants in her career and indeed any other activity. This represents tremendous progress compared with the fate of girls until relatively recently. But in developing countries, women often have fewer rights and less freedom. When it comes to international political power, women are totally outnumbered by men, accounting for fewer than 7 per cent of the world's leaders and only 24 per cent of lawmakers. And around the world, women still face discrimination, abuse and violence, simply on the basis of their sex.

Men and women, women and men: thousands of hours of research done and very few definite answers. It is important to always look past the headlines and our own biases. Both sexes have differences and similarities, advantages and disadvantages, challenges and opportunities. The one thing that's certain? Whether you're male or female, if you're reading this, you can at least be grateful that you're not a bony-eared assfish.

IDENTITY AND ORIENTATION

Humans, being the complex and wonderful species that we are, experience this big, wild world differently, and gender is no exception. Gender identity is a person's private sense and individual experience of their own gender – it is not just based on their anatomy. Psychologists tell us that gender identity is usually formed by the age of three and is difficult to change after that. Many factors influence our expression of our own personal gender identity, like the environment we grow up in and the behaviours we see around us.

How we understand and experience gender has become fluid – a person's sex may be male or female or, in rare cases, intersex based on their biology, but their gender might be different from their sex. A transgender person is someone whose gender identity does not match their sex assigned at birth. Some people feel so fundamentally different from their sex that they have hormone therapy and sometimes surgery to alter their bodies. For many people, describing themselves as a man or a woman wouldn't feel quite right. This area is complex and we don't yet understand it completely. One thing is clear: the issue of gender identity is now important for many people, and biology alone will not necessarily be able to answer it.

Sexual orientation is about who a person is romantically or sexually attracted to. Heterosexuality is a preference for persons of the opposite sex, homosexuality is a preference for one's own sex, while bisexuality is attraction to more than one sex. But again, attraction exists along a spectrum.

Sexual orientation has been a tricky topic for humans over the centuries. Many cultures throughout history punished people who were gay. Others, such as the ancient Greeks, were more tolerant. Some think that the first record of a homosexual couple was Khnumhotep and Niankhkhnum, ancient Egyptians

who lived around 2400 BC. They are depicted in a nose-kissing position, which was the most intimate pose in Egyptian art. Native Americans who were homosexual were seen as special shamans (religious leaders) with particular magical powers. There are many accounts of same-sex relationships in ancient Chinese literature. But in some cultures and religions it is still a difficult topic, because people have been taught to see it as 'different' and therefore unacceptable. However, homosexual behaviour is common throughout nature, appearing in mammals, reptiles, birds and insects.[4]

What might be the scientific basis for a person's sexuality? As ever with something as complex as this, their environment is one aspect, and biology is another. Once again – you'll get sick of hearing this – it's probably a combination of the two. There is a lot of evidence for sexuality being down to our genes. Much effort has gone into finding exactly how this works, but scientists are still not sure. It's likely that instead of one single gene, there is a combination of genetic markers that combine in a particular way. Exposure to certain hormones in the womb has also been shown to play a role. The overall view is that there will be biological factors behind sexual orientation, but these will be modified based on environmental and social factors.

There is a school of thought that asks: Why do we need to know the precise basis of gender or why someone is straight or gay? This is a reasonable point, as there is no obvious benefit from the

---

4 Jonathan, the world's oldest tortoise, had been mating with another tortoise named Frederica since 1991. In 2017, it was discovered that Frederica was actually probably male all along, and was renamed Frederic.

research being done in terms of, say, a new treatment for a disease. If a gene that predicts sexual orientation is found, why would that matter? Might people change that gene and alter their future? This is unlikely, as sexuality is probably much more complex than being determined by one or even a few gene variants.

The main reason people research this area is not to be patronising, but out of pure curiosity – to discover why things are the way they are. If we uncover the scientific basis for being straight or gay, or male or female or transgender, it could provide ammunition against those who try to discriminate against people who aren't like them. It can also help us understand each other better and realise that the battle of the sexes needn't be a battle at all.

The bottom line: Men and women have more in common than they do differences. There is huge diversity among humans and one thing that Mother Nature teaches us is that without diversity, species die out.

CHAPTER 8

WHY CAN'T WE JUST CHEER UP?

WE LIVE IN an age when, on the face of it, things have never been better. We have heated homes, flushing toilets, and easy access to food. Whole industries exist just to entertain us. Through the internet, we have access to all the knowledge of humankind, and endless pictures of cute baby animals. Men no longer spend every waking hour working in the fields, down coal mines, or dying in wars. Women, at least in Western countries, can now live almost as full a life as they want to.

And yet the number one fear of teenagers in a recent survey is of anxiety and depression. A large proportion of adults – as many as 18 per cent – have had serious depression at least once in their lives. And more college students are seeking help for mental health issues. In Ireland, almost 14,000 students asked for counselling in 2020–2021, up from 6,000 in 2010. Findings from research by the Royal College of Surgeons show that by the age of 13 years, one in three young people in Ireland are likely to have experienced some type of mental health difficulty.

Mental health is a serious problem that deserves our closest attention, given the amount of suffering it causes. But what exactly is going on in our brains? What happens when things go wrong? And what can we do to help?

CRAZY HISTORY

In the past, mental health problems were either ignored or misinterpreted because people didn't understand them. As we read in Chapter 2, the ancient Greeks thought that a person's mental state was driven by the balance of four fluids or 'humours' in their body: black bile, yellow bile, phlegm and blood. For depression, black bile was the one you didn't want out of kilter. The Greek word for black is *melan* – this gave us the word 'melancholia', which means deep sadness. The word humour (as in mood) comes from this idea. The Greeks also thought that many mental health issues in women could be traced back to a 'wandering womb' – a woman's uterus could come loose and float around the body. They also thought that it was attracted to nice smells and would flee from bad ones. Despite sounding silly (and painful), this theory stuck around for centuries, leading to the idea of 'hysteria', which comes from the Greek word for uterus. Helpfully, this covered everything from anxiety to increased appetite to disobedience. Nowadays, it's not recognised as a medical condition, but we do still use the word when someone is getting worked up – we say they're hysterical.

In the Middle Ages, mentally ill patients often became outcasts, left to their own devices in society. Often, people believed they were witches or possessed by demons. Exorcism, starvation and folk medicine were all used to treat people with mental illnesses. These ideas were about as useful as a hole in the head.[1]

Asylums began to appear in the sixteenth century, but they were meant to protect the public from the mentally ill, rather than actually

---

1 Sometimes literally – trepanation involved drilling a hole into a mentally ill person's skull to let the evil spirits out. A later treatment, lobotomy, involved removing part of the brain, often with an ice pick. If I need to remind you not to try this at home, you shouldn't be reading this book in the first place.

treat the patients. Most people in asylums were kept there against their will, lived in horrible conditions, and were often shown off to the public for a fee. As the scientific understanding of the brain increased, doctors began looking for ways to help patients get better. Psychological treatments were popularised by the likes of Sigmund Freud, who believed that a person's unconscious beliefs were the cause of mental illnesses. The first medications were developed in the mid-twentieth century, and slowly, treatments began to improve.

Nowadays, we know that mental illness is not caused by demons, or ghosts, or wandering wombs, but by something that is happening in our minds. We now know it is the mind that counts when it comes to mental health, and the mind is located in the brain. But we still don't know *what* the mind is. At its simplest, it's to do with neurons in our brains forming complex circuits, although neuroscientists warn us not to think of it as a computer. It's much more complicated than that! There are 100 billion neurons in your brain, all cracking and firing. Neurons connect to each other by releasing chemicals called neurotransmitters. These are like batons in a relay race with one runner (the neuron) passing the baton (the neurotransmitter) to the next runner. It is the dance between these neurons that is thought to explain things like memory, intelligence and personality, although we're still fairly unsure how this complex biochemical machine actually works. And we're even more clueless to what's going on when it turns against us, causing mental illness.

THE BLUES CLUB

You might not know who a lot of these people are, but there's a club that includes Caroline Aherne, Buzz Aldrin, Hans Christian Andersen, Marlon Brando, Kate Bush, Johnny Cash, Leonard Cohen, Charles Darwin, Charles Dickens, Bob Dylan, Stephen Fry, Lady Gaga, Martin Luther King, Stephen King, John Lennon, Abraham Lincoln, Spike Milligan, Jim Morrison, Morrissey, Wolfgang Amadeus Mozart, Isaac Newton, Dolores O'Riordan, Brad Pitt, Sylvia Plath, Edgar Allan Poe, Jackson Pollock, Sergei Rachmaninoff, Bruce Springsteen and Sting. And those are just my heroes. What do they all have in common? They've all had bouts of clinical depression.

So what exactly is depression? A depressed person will feel low and will not want to do the activities that they normally do. They will feel hopeless or worthless, lack energy and have trouble making decisions, and their appetite or sleep schedule might be disturbed. It's important to remember that we all feel like this at points in our life from time to time – these are normal feelings, and they pass. Feeling like this occasionally is part of the tapestry of emotions that makes us human. For depression to be diagnosed, these feelings have to keep coming back.

Although most people assume that depression is caused by a chemical imbalance in the brain, the evidence for this is actually poor. Some drugs do seem to help, but we're not sure why or how this works. Currently, brain chemistry and functioning let us down when it comes to a biological explanation for depression. No physical or blood test or scan can diagnose depression. This makes clinical trials for treatments difficult, because whether a treatment is working or not can only be evaluated by the patient. Patient reporting (which means a patient filling in a form) is a notoriously uncertain business. Sometimes, patients fill in a form incorrectly or exaggerate or downplay how they're feeling. And all the tester has to go on is the patient reporting on how they feel.

Another key area is the question of what causes depression in the first place. We have a much better idea what causes, say, infectious diseases, which are caused by bacteria or viruses, or type 1 diabetes, which is caused by lack of insulin, or cancer, which is caused by mutations in genes that control the growth of cells. Treatment can then be based on this knowledge. But for depression, the causes can be many and varied. Clearly, difficult life events play a major role. These events trigger a sense of loss, be it the loss of a loved one, our health, or our freedom. Or they make us worry, which gives rise to rumination – thinking too much – which then leads to a depressive episode. Studies have shown that genetics are also a factor – if you have a close family member who suffers from depression, you are more likely to suffer yourself. Like so many things, it is likely caused by a mixture of genetic and environmental factors. A person who already has a predisposition (a tendency to do or feel something) when faced with certain life experiences is more likely to have symptoms of depression.

Students are at a higher risk of depression. Risk factors are thought to include pressures linked to social media, personal and family expectations over academic success, and poor sleep quality. One study has found that almost 50 per cent of college students said that they woke up during the night to answer text messages. Poor sleep quality is a well-known risk factor for depression and anxiety, as is the use of drugs and alcohol. These drugs affect the brain, and during withdrawal, it is thought that the brain compensates for being disturbed, and this compensation can lead to depression.

ANXIOUS EVOLUTION

An interesting question is: Why hasn't a debilitating (serious) illness like depression disappeared over the generations? Why would a genetic tendency like this be passed on? It might be because our modern lives are so different from the conditions in which we evolved. Early *Homo sapiens* did not sit in front of a computer all day – they were too busy trying to survive. We also have access to endless amounts of doom and gloom through the 24-hour news channels. Through the internet, we are constantly being shown things that we don't have, which may make us less likely to be happy with what we do have. There is no question that our modern lifestyles are not helpful in promoting good mental health.

But that can't be the whole answer. Symptoms of depression have been found in every culture, including isolated societies, such as the Aché of Paraguay and the !Kung of southern Africa – societies where people are thought to live in environments similar to our evolutionary past. It's possible that when our ancient ancestors met and bred with Neanderthals, we picked up some genetic risk factors that came hand in hand with more helpful ones.[2] A study has found that Neanderthal DNA affects the risk of psychiatric disorders, including mood disorders and depression.

One theory as to why depression has survived is that depressed people often think intensely about their problems. These thoughts are called ruminations. They are persistent, and depressed people have difficulty thinking about anything else. They might dwell on a complex problem, breaking it down into smaller parts, which are then considered one at a time. Depression could be an adaptation that evolved to facilitate solving complex problems.

It is thought that anxiety might have similar evolutionary roots. One important theory about emotions is that they evolved to quickly organise our responses to our environment. For example, if we meet an angry tiger, we become fearful. That fear sharpens our senses, quickens our thinking, and activates our fight-or-flight response. Therefore, we don't have to consciously make ourselves

---

2 Neanderthal DNA sequences also include genes that affect skin, hair, fat metabolism, the risk of type 2 diabetes, cirrhosis, Crohn's disease, and – bizarrely – smoking addiction.

notice the danger of the tiger – we are instantly prepared to deal with it. People who were able to do this better clearly had an advantage in survival and reproduction, so were more likely to pass on this tendency.

Anxiety and fear are linked, so the organising power of anxiety is also important. But it can work overtime, and this becomes unhelpful – our brain sorts everyday situations into the 'dangerous' category, even when there is no angry tiger.[3] Our responses can be physiological (heart pounding, sweating), cognitive and emotional (thoughts about negative outcomes, rising worry), and behavioural (we avoid the perceived threat). Another theory is that the evolutionary advantage of anxiety could be that worrying about danger forces people to take fewer risks, seek safety, and focus on doing things well. This would make them more likely to survive and pass on their genes. In modern society, there are less immediate threats and more chronic and uncertain ones – it's not a sabre-toothed tiger that's the problem, but that horrible maths test on Friday – and so we feel more and more anxious in otherwise harmless situations.

---

3 If you *do* encounter an angry tiger, whatever you do, do not run, as running away from a tiger is inviting it to attack you. Slowly back away while standing up as tall as possible. Do not pee in the tiger's territory, although this may be difficult when facing down a 200 kg animal with claws as big as your head.

TALKING TREATMENT

One thing is certain: because anxiety and depression is becoming more common, especially among young people, and because it robs people of the joy of life, the disease needs our closest attention. Even though we might not know the exact cause, and even though we might not be able to measure things in the brain or body of someone who is suffering, everyone must be encouraged to seek support. Depression, like any other disease, can be helped.

For many people, depression eases with time, or we learn to live with the feelings we have – our brain adapts to the new circumstances. But some people need medical treatment and should be encouraged to get help. The first step should be a GP who can suggest the best way forward. Treatment might include therapy to explore difficult feelings. Cognitive behavioural therapy (CBT) has the most supporting evidence for treating both depression and anxiety. CBT consists of teaching patients to challenge their thinking patterns and also change counterproductive behaviour, and it appears to be very effective at preventing relapses. Medication called antidepressants may also help ease symptoms. In the USA, the Food and Drug Administration (FDA) did a review of clinical trials, which revealed that antidepressants stave off depression by 52 per cent overall, and a major study revealed that in 522 trials antidepressants were more effective than a placebo.

There are also some everyday things that lift people's mood and help stave off the dreaded black dog, as Winston Churchill used to call it. We're told that in order to be happy we actually need to

make an effort. This could be because our brains are inclined to default into worry and anxiety as a protective mechanism against harm. We're also inclined to overthink things, again probably as a survival mechanism. But we are not powerless. We can fight these tendencies. Some helpful behaviours are obvious, such as trying to maintain a positive outlook, hanging out with positive people and being part of a positive community. Regular exercise and enjoying the natural world have also been shown to help. In one enormous study involving 1.2 million people, on average people reported 3.4 days per month of poor mental health. This was reduced by 1.5 days in those who took regular exercise. Having a pet has also been shown to be really good for improving our mood (you can tell your parents that). Pets give us a focus, get us to take exercise and are an opportunity to socialise with others. Interacting with your pet dog has been shown to boost oxytocin, the love hormone, in both the dog and the owner. Volunteering can help too, as well as having a job that gives us meaning (which usually means a job that helps our fellow human beings). So there is hope – we just need to do a bit of hard work to get there. This can feel impossible when our emotions are overwhelming, so small steps are the way to go.

The bottom line: We've only got one life, and we must do everything we can to live it to the full and help those who are struggling. There are things we can do either to stave off depression or to stop it happening again. Tomorrow can always be better than today.

CHAPTER 9

WHY

DO

OTHERS

SCARE

US?

AS YOU SIT there reading this sentence, you are living in a body with a mind very similar to your ancestor who lived 200,000 years ago. Our species, *Homo sapiens sapiens* (or 'wise wise human' – so wise they named us twice), then lived on the plains of Africa with no smartphones, no nuclear weapons, no spaceships and no knowledge of DNA.

Around 90,000 years ago, a tribe of a few hundred people left those African plains and entered the Middle East. They stayed there a while, and then their descendants went off travelling again. Some of them went to Asia, some to Australia and some to the Americas. Forty thousand years ago, those left behind in the Middle East moved north to Europe. By about 10,000 years ago, every corner of the Earth was populated by the descendants of those people who left Africa.

The amazing thing is that we really haven't changed all that much over thousands of years. If we took someone from that time, brought them in a time machine to today, we could, with education, make them exactly like you and me. We could turn them into airline pilots or doctors or politicians. All that's happened since is that we've used the cleverness that we evolved way back then in all kinds of interesting ways.

FIGHTING TALK

Another thing that hasn't changed is our tendency to bicker. We've never been one big happy family. When different tribes met each other, they fought. Sometimes over resources, sometimes over people, and sometimes because the big voice in the sky told them to. Some clever human realised that putting a sharp rock on the end of a stick could be very useful, not just for hunting animals, but for poking holes in their neighbour. The most ancient record of a battle is from 14,000 years ago in northern Sudan, where skeletons have been found with wounds from spears or arrows. Fighting began to show up in cave paintings around 10,000 years ago. We discovered metal and started using it to make all sorts of interesting (and painful) weapons like knives, swords and axes.

We kept on bickering: the ancient Greeks fought, the Romans fought, the Egyptians fought. In Ireland, the earliest battle dates from about 2500 BCE (although some sources say that no one was killed or wounded in this battle as it was fought by magic). In the Middle Ages, people began to build castles to protect themselves and used gunpowder to develop better and stronger weapons. Ships set sail from Europe, and this meant that different branches of the human family reunited, first in the Americas, and later in Australia.

In both cases, the invaders killed the locals, either directly or by spreading diseases like smallpox, which the natives had no immunity to. Europe was almost constantly at war from the Dark Ages on, with the fighting leading to World Wars I and II, which would leave whole generations of young men dead.[1]

What could have possibly justified all that killing? After all, these warring tribes are all descended from the first tribe that left Africa. Sure, every family has rows over the Christmas table, but this is ridiculous. Why do we hate each other so? Why do others frighten us? Why can't we just get along?

SUSPICIOUS MINDS

The instinct to be suspicious of others seems to be hardwired into our brains. Most of our behaviour is driven by the need to pass on our DNA, and our family shares some of this DNA, so if they are threatened, we will defend them – after all, blood is thicker than water. Early humans would have lived in small groups of maybe a hundred or so. Think of it like a small Irish village: you know everyone and you are related to half of them, so it's in your interest to defend them.

Tribes have always identified themselves as being different from neighbouring groups: the O'Reillys in the next village over

---

1 In recent years, we have replaced some of the fighting with sports, so players can bash it out on the playing field rather than on the battlefield. In Europe, we try to do our fighting over something possibly even more terrible: the Eurovision Song Contest.

are eejits, not like the sensible people in your village. And their football team is obviously much worse than yours, and if they somehow manage to win a match, they're cheats. In ancient Greece, anyone not from Greece was a 'barbarian' – someone to be hated and not trusted (just like those O'Reillys). We're hardwired to think that we're better than outsiders. This tendency often rears its ugly head through acts of racism – the fear or hatred of a race based on the belief that your own race is superior. But you might be surprised to learn that the whole idea of race in the first place is fairly new.

It began in the eighteenth century, when Europeans began to travel and come into contact with groups from different continents. Christopher Columbus encountered Native Americans, and later, in Australia, Captain Cook came across Aboriginal Australians.[2] To European eyes, these people looked very different, so the explorers decided they must be a different race, and they grouped them together based on skin colour and physical differences. In 1735, the scientist Carl Linnaeus went further, dividing the human species into four races: *europaeus, asiaticus, americanus* and *africanus*. And, of course, the Europeans had to come out on top of the pile – Linnaeus described *Homo sapiens europaeus* as being active and adventurous, while *Homo sapiens africanus* was said to be crafty, lazy and careless. Many scientists believed that different races had actually evolved separately in each continent and had no shared ancestor. Classifications like these were used to justify the slaughter of native

---

2 To say this did not end well for the Native Americans and Aboriginal Australians is an understatement.

people, and the bloody business of slavery. This led to horrifying acts of violence – millions of people dead or stolen from their homes, transported to different continents and worked, often to death.

The belief that some humans were worth less than others continued into the twentieth century when eugenics became popular. Eugenics was the idea that the human race could be improved by letting certain people reproduce and stopping others from doing so. The most famous eugenics programme was that of the Nazis, who wanted to improve the so-called Aryan race, which the Nazis believed they belonged to. Jewish, Romani, disabled and LGBT people were all killed in huge numbers. In the USA, eugenics programmes sterilised people who were thought to be weak or unfit.[3] The races were to be kept separate: it was a crime to marry someone from a different race up until 1967.

All of this cruelty was driven by the (false) belief that humans are divided into races that are fundamentally different. This 'scientific racism' was used to promote terrible policies and cause tremendous suffering. This should serve as a warning: having blind faith in science can be dangerous. If tomorrow an experiment proved that people from Galway are naturally better drivers than people from Cork, it wouldn't be right to take the cars away from the Corkonians and give them to the Galwegians. Black and white thinking like this has caused many of the worst chapters in human history. Science

---

3 John Harvey Kellogg was a prominent American eugenicist. Why does that name seem familiar? Well, you might have seen it on your breakfast table. John Harvey Kellogg's company was responsible for inventing corn flakes. Tomorrow's breakfast might not seem so sweet …

should be used as a tool, not as a religion or political system, because *nothing* in life is ever black or white. Modern science has hugely improved human life, but human life involves much more than science can know or improve.

END OF THE RACE

An example of human cooperation rather than division was the Human Genome Project. This involved scientists from around the world working together to discover the exact set of DNA that controls the way human beings develop and grow. This is known as the genome. The sequence the scientists described didn't come from a single person – it was a patchwork made up of the genomes of lots of people. Because of this, the scientists could learn many things about the entire human race.

One of the most important things they found is that 99.9 per cent of one human's genome is identical to any other human's genome. People might have superficial differences (such as skin colour or a fold of skin around the eyes) but under the surface we are all very similar. This tiny variation between different people does not support the idea of genetically distinct races. There are bigger physical differences within one ethnic group than between groups. Any physical differences we *do* have follow what geneticists call a 'cline' – a change in a trait across a geographical range.

Take skin colour as an example. When humans left Africa, they all had dark skin, which helped them use the sun's light to make vitamin D, which is important for our bodies. People then moved north into environments with less sunlight. A genetic mutation caused light skin to appear, which allowed people to make enough vitamin D in their skin from the weaker sunlight. The people with this genetic mutation were more likely to survive in these shady places, and they passed this trait down to their children. Nowadays, there is a cline from Northern Europe southwards to the Mediterranean and down into Africa. At one end, skin colour is pale white, and at the other it is dark, with skin colour getting darker as we move down the cline. The same applies to most other physical traits – there's no obvious boundary where a trait suddenly changes.

What all of this means is the idea of 'race' is now no longer scientifically acceptable. It is seen as a social construct, a meaning put on something by a society. Think of it like a country – there's no big line in the sand that separates the USA from Mexico (despite the best efforts of some recent presidents). Both countries just agreed to imagine the border in a certain place. And, like borders, our ideas of race are always changing – for example, amazing as it seems, Irish and Italian people weren't considered to be members of the white race until fairly recently.

Social scientists now prefer to talk about 'ethnicity' – a group that shares a culture, ancestry and history. While people may have different ethnic backgrounds, there's no biology behind separating people by race. We're all just one big human family. This might sound like something you'd hear on *Sesame Street* – but it's true!

BREAKING THE CYCLE

Surprisingly – or maybe unsurprisingly – people don't often listen to scientists. All over the world, people are still judged on the basis of their apparent race rather than as individuals, which leads to inequality and suffering.

Racists might argue that a certain type of people are dirty. They follow a strange and dangerous religion. They take our jobs and lower our wages. They drink, fight and are no better than animals. These are all arguments you might hear when people talk about foreigners, especially in dark corners of the internet and at family gatherings (everybody has that one uncle). But at one time in history, these were all descriptions of the Irish people, who were often discriminated against as immigrants. Remember: as the singer Imelda May says, 'You don't get to be racist and Irish.'

Ireland has a strong history of trying to combat racism. In 2005 Ireland was one of the first countries in the world to develop a National Action Plan against Racism, which ran for four years. The Irish government has a number of initiatives, including programmes to promote intercultural awareness and to actively combat racism. Unfortunately, one area that is often overlooked is discrimination against the Traveller community. Irish Travellers are an ethnic and cultural minority, whose roots in the country go back centuries, but members of this community are still being discriminated against in Ireland.

Racial stereotypes are exaggerated mental pictures we have of a particular set of people. These ideas mean that people are set up to be racist the first time they meet someone of a different ethnicity – if you believe a certain group of people is lazy or violent, you will see their behaviour as lazy or violent. This is one reason why it is so important that people of different backgrounds appear in our books, television shows and films. The more you know about something, the less frightening it is. Plus, learning about other ethnicities is fun – each one has a rich history and culture (and usually delicious food).

Putting aside the rights and wrongs, having people of different ethnicities in a local area or a country benefits local and national economies. When Donald Trump tried to ban Muslims and Syrians from coming to the USA, he was reminded that Steve Jobs had a

Syrian immigrant father. No immigrants = no iPhones = no tweeting! Many sportspeople, like Olympic medallist Mo Farah, came to the UK after conflict in their home countries. In Ireland, politician Leo Varadkar's father was an immigrant from Mumbai, India.

Immigrants and the children of immigrants are often entrepreneurs or own businesses. They grow the workforce and are often highly qualified and skilled as well as being essential for establishing new businesses. Far from taking jobs, immigrants create jobs. And they are also consumers: they buy goods and services with the wages they earn, and that creates jobs for others, including for local workers.

Despite this, racism remains a major issue, both in Ireland and more widely, and there has been a nasty increase in this kind of thinking over the last few years. Around the world, racist leaders try to prey on our suspicious and fearful instincts. It's very easy for a politician to say, 'Look over there! That person looks different from you, aren't they scary? They're the reason your bills are so high and why you keep stubbing your toe every morning!' When we hear things like this, our brains agree – as we learned earlier, we're hardwired to think that way. The problem is that we aren't living in the wild any more. If we lived the way we did back then, we'd all be dead from curable diseases, we'd freeze to death in winter, and we'd have to eat all our food raw and without ketchup. While our instincts are helpful, they can be hurtful too, and we need to recognise when they're not being useful.

There is hope: there is a global trend towards less discrimination. Young people are much less racist than older generations, and they continue to become more tolerant and accepting of difference. We can fight back against the evils of racism through education and communication. Diversity is great for society at every level, from culture and learning to business and economic growth.

The bottom line: There is no need to fear our neighbours any more. Racism is an evil with no basis in science. There are small differences between every human, and these should be valued. But deep down, we are all the same.

CHAPTER 10

WHY

IS OUR

WORLD

SO

UNEQUAL?

I N 2022, THE world's population reached eight billion people. That's an eight with nine zeros after it: 8,000,000,000. If you started now, it would take you 800 years to count every one of those eight billion people. This number is so huge that it is hard for us to imagine. It might be easier if we instead think of the world's population as 100 people.

If there were 100 people on the planet:

- 14 people would not have learned how to read and write, and 93 people would not have a college or university degree.
- 22 people would not have a home that protects them from wind and rain.
- 9 people would not have access to clean, safe drinking water.
- 11 people would not have enough good, nutritious food to eat.
- 1 person would be dying from starvation.

If you are reading this book, you are probably one of the lucky ones.

It gets worse: Half of the world's net worth (money and assets) belongs to 1 per cent of the world's population. The richest 22 men in the world have more wealth than all the women in Africa. Worldwide, men own 50 per cent more wealth than women. The top 10 per cent of people have 85 per cent of all the wealth; the other 90 per cent have the remaining 15 per cent.

Nothing much seems to have changed over thousands of years. In the past, a tiny minority held all the riches and lorded it over the peasants, who were forced to scrape by. The invention of agriculture seems to be partly to blame for this. The ruling class had the seeds, the land, the know-how and the power to control the production of food. They made the less smart or less able or less well-connected people in their community work for them, but didn't share out the profits equally.

Occasionally, people would rise up to try to make things more equal, but things usually ended up with the rich and powerful back on top. During the French Revolution, the people decided to chop the heads off their useless nobility, but then Napoleon came along and declared himself Emperor. The Romans knew that if the workers were given 'bread and circuses' (like exciting gladiator fights), they would keep working and not rebel. Perhaps the equivalent of all this today is a tasty takeaway delivered right to your door and reality TV on Netflix.

Today, the planet is more divided than it has ever been before. The rich keep getting richer, and the poor keep getting poorer. How can this be? Why don't the top 1 per cent give up some of their wealth and spread the money around more evenly, especially when they know that many millions of people are suffering from poverty? And what about those of us who have more money than we need? Why don't we give up a lot of that wealth to others? Are we all basically greedy or is there something else going on? What can we do to fix the inequality that exists in our world?

A BUNDLE OF BILLIONAIRES

Let's go back to that big number from the start of the chapter: 8 billion. For a bit of perspective, think about it this way: one million seconds is about 11.5 days. One billion seconds is more than 31 *years*. If you, and one descendent per generation, saved €100 every day, and each of you lived for 90 years, it would take you and 304 generations of your descendants to save up one billion euro. A billion really is an extraordinarily huge amount of money.

What would you do with a billion dollars? Would you buy a private jet? Your own personal island? All of that would only use up a tiny fraction of your wealth. If you're a billionaire, a trip on a private jet is the same price as a bus journey for a normal person. Buying a restaurant is the same as buying a meal. You would have to work pretty hard to spend all that money (although most people would be willing to give it a go).

As of 2022, there were 3,311 billionaires in the world. Most of them are worth $10 billion or less (poor things). After that, 5 per cent are worth between $10 billion and $30 billion, while mega-billionaires are worth more than $30 billion. Some of these people are so rich that they had to invent a new number to describe how much money they have: Jeff Bezos, who founded Amazon, hit a net worth of $120 billion in 2022 and is now known as a centibillionaire.[1] Among the rest of the top five are Elon Musk (CEO of Tesla and Twitter) and Bill Gates (founder of Microsoft). In Ireland, Patrick and John Collison (founders of the payment system Stripe) top the list.

What type of people become billionaires? Ninety per cent are men, but the trend for women has risen in the last five years. Around a dozen world leaders are billionaires, and there are about a hundred billionaires in the Chinese parliament. The most likely way to make a billion-dollar fortune: go into finance and investments. Next comes manufacturing, then fashion and retail. But some people have earned their way to the top in unusual ways, like brewing kombucha and breeding pigs.

Worryingly, the earnings of billionaires skyrocketed during the COVID-19 pandemic. The world's ten richest men more than doubled their fortunes from $700 billion to $1.5 trillion – at a rate of $15,000 per second or $1.3 billion a day – during the first two years of a pandemic that saw the incomes of 99 per cent of humanity fall and over 160 million more people forced into poverty.

The mega-rich certainly have plenty of money to give away. But do they?

---

1 But he's not the richest person of all time. That title goes to oil magnate John D. Rockefeller, who became a US billionaire in 1916, which makes him history's wealthiest person, if we adjust his wealth to today's money.

GIVE IT AWAY NOW

Charity involves giving time or money to those in need. The word 'charity' comes from the Latin *caritas*, which describes a particular form of love for your fellow humans.[2] But when you're a billionaire, you need a better word to describe how you give your money away. This is the world of philanthropy, which is different from charity, as philanthropy tries to get at the root cause of a problem. The difference is described in the well-known saying: 'If you give a man a fish, you feed him for a day. If you teach a man to fish, you feed him for a lifetime.' Philanthropists generally try to teach a man to fish, if you know what I mean.

First, the good news. There has been an upward trend in philanthropy over the past decade, which goes along with the increasing number of billionaires. According to the Wealth-X Billionaire Census, this is due to increased awareness of global environmental and social issues, a more diverse and multi-generational billionaire population, and 'consternation over rising inequality'. Nice to know that some billionaires, at least, are feeling consternation! The numbers show that, globally, the top 20 billionaires donated 0.8 per cent of their total wealth in 2018. Not much, is it? But it's a start.

When we look at where the money goes, we see some interesting trends. Education comes out on top. Two-thirds of billionaires give money to scholarships, educational support, outreach programmes

2 Not to be confused with *carnitas,* which is Mexican pulled pork. If you ran a charity burrito restaurant, you could call it *Caritas Carnitas.*

and teacher training. Healthcare comes in next, with 14 per cent of donations. Ten per cent goes to arts, culture and sports, and 8 per cent is donated to environmental issues (that figure will likely increase with the recent awareness of climate change). Finally, 5 per cent goes to religious organisations.

Health issues are squarely in the sights of these mega-rich people. Mark Zuckerberg, founder of Facebook, has set aside $3 billion to 'cure, prevent or manage' disease. A large proportion of Bill Gates's money has been spent on vaccine development and global health. A project funded by the Gates Foundation in 2001 gave $70 million to develop a vaccine for meningitis A and make it affordable for everyone who needs it. A successful vaccine was developed at a cost of 50 cents per dose. By 2013, less than a decade after a meningitis outbreak had killed 25,000 people, only four cases have been reported. The reason the vaccine programme succeeded was because of long-term funding and a hands-off approach by the Gates Foundation – they gave money to the experts and let them get on with it.

Some billionaires are even looking past medical issues to the end of the line. A growing number have decided they want to use their enormous wealth to try to help humans cheat death. Some of the techniques they've invested in include:

- transfusing blood from young, healthy people into older people
- cryonics, the science of freezing yourself to be thawed out later
- digitally uploading your brain to the cloud so you can live for ever
- space travel and colonising other planets.

All of this seems good (except for, perhaps, the blood transfusions): lots of money is being invested into good(ish) causes. But there is criticism, especially in the USA, where governments used to collect billions from the wealthiest people and then democratically redistribute the money. This is happening less and less. We now have a scenario where the wealthiest pay less tax than before and then donate their money however they like. There is no clear way to assess whether the money is being spent effectively or on the right things. A person could donate a huge amount of money to researching a cure for hiccups – but would this be a good use of funds? Is it right to think about colonising other planets when so many are suffering here on Earth?

There are calls for higher taxes on the mega-wealthy to make them pay their fair share. Perhaps surprisingly, some are even in favour of this! In 2022, a group of more than a hundred of the world's richest people called on governments to make them pay more tax. The group, who called themselves the Patriotic Millionaires, said

that a wealth tax could raise much-needed funds around the world. According to economist Jeffrey Sachs, the cost of ending poverty is roughly $175 billion each year for 20 years. This means that the world's billionaires – currently worth a combined sum of $12.7 trillion – could solve world poverty and still have almost $10 trillion left to spare. This is unlikely to happen anytime soon.

But there was an interesting development in the world of philanthropy in 2010 when Bill and Melinda Gates and Warren Buffet (then the world's number one and number two in terms of wealth) started the Giving Pledge. The aim of this campaign was to get wealthy people to donate at least half their wealth, in their lifetime or in their will, to charitable causes. Initially, 40 people signed up, all in the USA. As of 2022, the number had risen to 236, from 28 different countries. Not bad going, if it happens. According to its website, the Giving Pledge was inspired by the example set by 'millions of people at all income levels, who gave generously – and often at great personal sacrifice – to make the world better'. This is interesting, as it suggests that what Gates is trying to do is guilt the hugely wealthy into giving more – if poorer people can do it, then you should too. Here's hoping the number of sign-ups keeps growing.

If inequality keeps increasing, well, remember the French Revolution? At the time, political philosopher Jean-Jacques Rousseau said: 'When the people shall have nothing more to eat, they will eat the rich.' In September 2011, hundreds of activists gathered in Manhattan for the first day of the Occupy Wall Street Movement – a weeks-long sit-in in New York City's financial district protesting against income inequality and corporate (business) corruption. Since then, protests have continued around the world. People are becoming more aware of inequality and unfairness and are fighting back. Young people are the main drivers of this movement, so there may yet be real change. If not, well, there's always the guillotine.

NATURAL BORN GIVERS

Whatever about the mega-rich, what about the general public? A major recent study has pulled together 500 studies to examine the key factors that drive giving. For 85 per cent of donations, the main reason for giving was 'I was asked.' This might seem obvious enough, but it doesn't answer why the donor chose to say yes to a specific charity. Most people give because of their personal values, which include compassion to those in need. Donors also report that giving makes them feel good or makes them look good in the eyes of others. Overall, though, people are more likely to be motivated by helping others rather than getting something back.

Can money buy happiness? It can, if you're giving it away. A Chinese proverb says: 'If you want happiness for an hour, take a nap. If you want happiness for a day, go fishing. If you want happiness for a year, inherit a fortune. If you want happiness for a lifetime, help somebody.'

The science backs this up: studies consistently show that donations to charitable organisations can have a lasting positive impact on your mood. When you give money to a cause you believe in, your brain activity changes. Scientists can observe through brain imaging studies how giving to charity generates increased activity in the brain's reward system. In fact, there are two areas of the brain that become more active when a person gives money to charity. The first is the same area that distributes the feel-good dopamine chemicals associated with money and food. Giving, then, is truly a natural high. The second area activated by charitable giving is the area of the brain that helps form social attachment. In an age where isolation and loneliness are all too common, giving to charity reminds us that we're all interconnected and need to support each other. Human beings have survived as a species because we have evolved the ability to care for those in need and to cooperate.

Let's finish up by looking at the origin of the word 'philanthropy', which means love of humankind. It comes from the ancient Greek play *Prometheus Bound*. In the play, the first humans live in dark caves and have no language or tools or culture. Zeus, the powerful king of the gods, thinks these creatures are worthless and wants to destroy them. Another god, Prometheus, decides to help the poor cave dwellers out by giving them two incredibly powerful gifts: fire (knowledge) and optimism (hope). The first ever philanthropic gifts were knowledge and hope – now that's powerful stuff.

The bottom line: Whether you're a big earner or on an average income, we should all be aiming for a more equal society. If everyone gives what they can, it is possible.

CHAPTER 11

WHY ARE WE WRECKING THE PLANET?

THIS STORY BEGINS millions of years ago, on a young, green planet. It was quiet – there were no honking cars or noisy factories – and the skies were clear of smog. The seas were filled with billions of microscopic creatures called zooplankton and algae. Their bodies were full of carbon, which they had absorbed from carbon dioxide in the air. When these tiny life forms died, they settled at the bottom of the sea, where they were covered up with silt and mud over millions of years. As the pressure grew, they slowly turned into a liquid that we now call petroleum. Millions of years later, if you were lucky enough to live over these lakes of underground petroleum, you would become enormously rich. Because petroleum became one of the most sought-after things in the world.

Since ancient times, it's been known that petroleum (also known as crude oil) could be used as fuel. The Chinese used it in the fourth century, while the Japanese described it as 'burning water' in the seventh century. The modern history of petroleum began in the nineteenth century when James Young, a Scottish chemist, distilled a light, thin oil from crude oil. Burning it gave off heat and light, which was incredibly useful. Soon, it was powering street lamps, and when the internal combustion engine was invented, cars appeared on the roads and the oil industry really took off.

Oil is what's known as a fossil fuel – because, funnily enough, it is fuel made up of fossils. Coal is another fossil fuel, made up of ancient plants that decayed over millions of years into peat, and then into coal. Those decaying plants, like the tiny creatures that form oil, are also full of carbon. Fossil fuels have been responsible for huge leaps forward in human history. Using them, people could easily heat their houses and fuel their trains, planes and automobiles. The process of refining fossil fuels also creates lots of chemicals, which could be used to make other things like fertiliser, meaning food was much more plentiful. Plastic, made from another by-product of oil, changed the world, as cheap, long-lasting products became available for everyone.

But it's not all good news. It turns out that burning oil or coal releases the carbon that was trapped in the bodies of those ancient microscopic creatures and plants. This carbon, in the form of CO_2, is returned to the air. And that's when the trouble begins. The story that started with those teeny tiny creatures is still ongoing, but it's taken a darker turn. If we don't do something, it will have an unhappy ending – unhappy for us, and unhappy for the entire planet. How could this happen? And what can we all do about it?

GREENHOUSE GROOVE

It's all down to the greenhouse effect. Think of a regular greenhouse: the sun shines in through the glass and warms the air, but the glass prevents a lot of the heat escaping, so the temperature in the greenhouse goes up. Instead of glass, the Earth has an atmosphere surrounding the entire planet. Gases in the atmosphere absorb heat from the sun and then radiate it all around them, including to the surface of the Earth, which then warms up.

The natural greenhouse effect is critical for much of life on Earth – if it didn't happen, our planet would be too cold and the oceans would be frozen solid. The evolution of complex life would not have been possible without it, as the conditions needed to be just right for cells to emerge. The greenhouse effect, however, has become our enemy: because of it, the Earth is getting too damn hot.

In the late nineteenth century, scientists began arguing that human emissions of greenhouse gases could change the climate. Throughout the twentieth century, scientists began to gather data, a firestorm of data, all of which was saying the same thing – the Earth's temperature was indeed rapidly rising. This could only be explained by the increase in the greenhouse gas CO_2.

Ice core data is especially important for understanding what the climate was like in the past. This is a sample of ice removed from high mountain glaciers or polar ice caps. The ice builds up year on year, so scientists can take samples and analyse them to find out what the composition of the air was a long time ago, even as far back as 800,000 years. The ice cores reveal that CO_2 has been on the up and up since the early 1800s, when we first began burning fossil fuels. The current level of CO_2 is at its highest for five million years, and almost half of the increase has happened since 1990. The last time CO_2 levels were this high, the Earth's average temperature was 3°C warmer. Greenland was actually green, and parts of Antarctica had forests. The sea level was 20 metres higher than today, which would mean no Dublin, London, New York, Boston or San Francisco.

Fossil fuels aren't the only culprit. Agriculture also produces greenhouse gas emissions from livestock and fertilisers. As cows and sheep digest their food, they produce methane. It is estimated that 90 per cent of methane is expelled in the breath of animals with the remainder a product of flatulence. This is all a fancy way of saying that cow burps and farts are even more deadly than your dad's silent stinkers. And there are about 1 billion cows on the planet, all to provide meat and dairy for us to eat – that's a lot of methane. Methane has more than 80 times the warming power of carbon dioxide over the first 20 years after it reaches the atmosphere. Even though CO_2 has a longer-lasting effect, methane sets the pace for warming in the short term. At least 25 per cent of today's global warming is driven by methane from human actions.

The Earth has its own built-in system of managing these dangerous gases. Plants and trees can act like a sink – they absorb CO_2 from the atmosphere and produce that all-important oxygen. But we've been chopping down 10 million hectares of trees every year to make space to grow crops and rear livestock, and to produce materials like paper. A hectare is about as big as an international rugby union field, and we're losing 10 *million* of them a year, mostly in the tropical rainforests.

And then there are our oceans. They provide us with food, 85 per cent of the oxygen we breathe, and also regulate the climate. They absorb an amazing 90 per cent of the heat from the warming atmosphere and soak up many gigatonnes of CO_2. Without the ocean's surface, temperatures on Earth would be 30°C warmer and there wouldn't be much life. And billions of plankton float through the oceans, taking energy from the sun to use in photosynthesis and releasing oxygen. They are responsible for half of all the oxygen on Earth – the other half comes from land plants.

But our lovely oceans are in trouble too: their temperature has increased by 0.4°C since 1969. That doesn't seem like much, you might think – not even enough to make you take off your jumper. But every bit of warming, no matter how small, has devastating effects. The Greenland and Antarctic ice sheets are melting because of the temperature rise. Antarctica is losing about 150 billion tonnes of ice per year, and Greenland is losing about 280 billion tonnes of ice per year. That's enough to fill over 400 billion swimming pools – every year.

Overall, the sea level rose by 20 cm in the last century, bringing the threat of flooding to places near sea level. About 680 million people live in coastal communities, which will be flooded by the rising sea levels. A further five million live in the arctic region and 65 million live on small islands that are at risk of going under. All of these people may lose their homes, drinking water and livelihoods. Many are in poor communities. Reports predict that extreme floods, which used to hit once per century, will happen every year from 2050.

Melting ice caps will also lead to more freshwater. This mightn't seem like such a big problem, but our ocean currents depend on salty water, so upsetting this means that existing currents go haywire. For example, the Gulf Stream is a current that gives Ireland its mild climate, and if it were to stop flowing, dramatic climate change would happen.

The increase in CO_2 is also leading to the oceans becoming more acidic. This is affecting life in the oceans, particularly the coral reefs, which don't like an acidic environment. Many species of fish will be unable to survive the warming waters and the oceans will become less productive. An incredible three billion of us rely on seafood as our number one source of protein.

All in all, the picture is looking pretty bleak. The planet Venus shows us what can happen when there is a runaway greenhouse effect. There, CO_2 levels from rocks and soil built up in the atmosphere millions of years ago. The warming of the planet led to more CO_2 being released until eventually the atmosphere was 96 per cent CO_2. Eventually, all the surface water boiled off and the surface temperature is currently a fairly toasty 462°C.[1] The Earth is heading in a similar direction.

CONSPIRACY THINKING

But there are always people willing to stick their head in the sand and ignore the problem. Many are still in denial – Donald Trump even tweeted that global warming is a hoax invented by the Chinese. You might even have a few naysayers in your own family. Here are a few false claims you might hear – and the truth.

---

1 The surface of Venus isn't somewhere you'd like to be. It has temperatures that can melt lead, an atmosphere so thick it would crush you, and clouds of sulphuric acid that smell like rotten eggs to top it off. Despite that, there are some probes heading that way in the next decade, with great names like VERITAS, DAVINCI, HAVOC and VAMP.

'**Climate change is part of a natural cycle.**' Yes, there are natural weather cycles – el Niño, which brings storms in the Pacific Ocean, is one example. But the changes that are happening are too big and too fast to be natural. Climate scientists look at long-term patterns and they're all saying the same thing.

'**Life will find a way to survive.**' It might – but we are losing plant and animal species at an alarming rate, which is changing the ecology of the entire planet. And humans are not equipped to deal with drought and floods. It might just be extremely durable species that survive – Earth might become Planet of the Cockroaches.

'**If the planet is warming, why is it raining/snowing so much?**' Climate is different from weather. Weather is short-term patterns, while climate is what happens over a much longer period. The warming of the Earth can cause the short-term weather to act strangely, but the long-term patterns all point to the same thing – it's getting hot, hot, hot.

'**Scientists can't agree on the cause.**' Ninety-seven per cent of climate scientists have concluded that we are the cause of this problem, and burning fossil fuels is the primary reason. This is an extremely high level of agreement, considering that scientists love to bicker among themselves until the truth is reached. It's not at 100 per cent because some scientists prefer to be mavericks and go against prevailing evidence (or incorrectly fill in the questionnaire).[2] But it is

---

2 If you threw 1,000 scientists out a window, at least one of them would argue against gravity the entire way down. But please don't try.

now undeniable. It is beyond all reasonable doubt that global warming is being caused by greenhouse gases emitted because of human activity.

'It's all a big conspiracy – scientists are all in it for the money.' First, scientists are terrible at keeping secrets – they're much more likely to shout their results from the rooftops. Second, it would be much more profitable for scientists to put on a happy face and take pay cheques from the fossil fuel companies.

So, now that we've got those conspiracy theories out of the way, let's talk solutions.

CHANGING COURSE

Trying to slow climate change is a bit like trying to get a supertanker to do a rapid U-turn. It's hard work, slow going and it will take time for the effects to filter down. The goal is to reverse the emissions that occurred over the twentieth century. It will mean replacing everything that burns oil, gas or coal. It will mean recycling or replacing all plastics (which are made from petroleum). It will mean transforming farms all over the world. And all this needs to be done while economies expand to meet the needs of a population that by 2100 will be 50 per cent larger than today.

Only international action will work. If one country reduces emissions, but everyone else doesn't, the risks for the planet remain the same. And if one country doesn't reduce emissions and all the others do, then that country will benefit without putting the effort in. A recent study found that as few as 100 companies were responsible for 70 per cent of global emissions. Those companies need to be targeted and encouraged to change. But we can't blame them and let ourselves off the hook – we buy the products that they produce, driving demand. We need to change our ways while pressuring them to change theirs.

Because the processes that are causing climate change are fundamental to the world economy, the ways of stopping it will need to be all-encompassing. Saving the planet may actually involve 'degrowth': stop aeroplane travel, stop eating meat, ban private cars and divert money from consumption to building infrastructure that is green. We need to make sure there's a just transition – greening the economy in a way that is as fair and inclusive as possible, creating decent work opportunities and leaving no one behind.

Most important, there must be a shift towards sources of renewable energy. Currently 7 per cent of the world's energy comes from the wind and the sun, the two main renewable energy sources. Solar power is an obvious thing to invest in – the sun provides free energy, if we can figure out how to use it efficiently. Wind is a perfect complement to solar power, as it blows during the night as well as during the day and is stronger in winter, when there is less sun.[3]

Another approach is negative emissions, or taking CO_2 out of the atmosphere. We already have a great way to do this: plants. They suck up CO_2 and use it in photosynthesis to make more of themselves. We need a lot more plants and trees, and we definitely need to stop cutting down what we have left. We must also make

---

3 What's a wind turbine's favourite colour? Blew.

sure that the plankton in our oceans continue to thrive and grow, as they are great carbon-eaters.

Our oceans are filling up with waste plastic. Every minute, the equivalent of one garbage truck of plastic is dumped into our oceans. Every minute! Of this, 236,000 tonnes become microplastics, pieces of plastic smaller than your little fingernail. Many fish we eat, including mackerel and sea trout, have microplastics in their bodies. There are five enormous plastic patches in the oceans – the one between California and Hawaii is the size of the state of Texas. Some of the plastic in the patch is over 50 years old, and includes things like toothbrushes, water bottles, pens, mobile phones and plastic bags. Overall, it contains approximately 5 kg of plastic for every 1 kg of plankton. If we don't stop plastic entering the oceans, by 2050 there will be more plastic than fish by weight in our oceans. Think about those plastic patches every time you reach for something in a shop.

Yet technology might get the tide to turn on plastics in our oceans. The plastic often comes from rivers, which sweep tonnes of waste from the land out to sea. A company called Ichthion has invented a device that sits on the surface of rivers. It diverts floating objects to the riverbank, then a conveyor belt lifts them out, a camera reads them and then transfers anything plastic into waste bins. It can sort up to 80 tonnes of plastic per day, which is sent off for reuse or recycling. There's another device that can be attached to ships and filter plastic particles from the ocean. We might still win the battle against plastics in our oceans.

Scientists are also coming up with 'super corals' by cross-breeding species that are better able to handle warm waters with others that can't, producing heat-tolerant hybrids. This approach is a way of buying time to save corals – but the oceans will have to cool a bit to be sure corals survive. Another important approach is to establish marine reserves to protect species, including fish.

So there's hope. There has to be hope.

A CLEANER FUTURE

Apart from the governments and politicians (who we already know can be pretty useless), change will come from one other place: all of us. Why we continue to wreck the planet is a complicated question, tied into our greed, laziness and the needs of the global economy. What will it take for us to change? We are being told to help the planet by changing our personal choices when it comes to things like diet, travel (especially air travel), energy use in our homes, what we buy in our shops and even the size of our families. To meet the climate change target, we must aim to each produce fewer than three tonnes of CO_2 per year. Currently, the average person in the EU emits 11 tonnes of CO_2 per year. In Ireland, the average is 13 tonnes.

There is also hope in a success story for an environmental policy shift that happened in the 1990s. This began in 1985, when climatologists reported a large decrease in ozone levels over the Antarctic. Ozone is a gas that occurs in a layer above the Earth. It is important because it filters UV light (ultraviolet light) that comes from the sun and can be damaging. The reduction of the ozone layer was worrying because UV light can cause cancer. It was then shown that the loss of ozone was being caused by chemicals called chlorofluorocarbons (CFCs), which were used in aerosol cans and refrigerants. This led to an international agreement to ban CFCs, and now the ozone hole is recovering. This is a major success story for global environmental policy.

We also caught a glimpse of what a clean, healthy world might look like during the COVID-19 pandemic. The huge decrease in human activity led to the air clearing over many countries, with levels of CO_2 and nitrogen dioxide plummeting. The greenhouse effect can then be lessened, and there can be cleaner air, since nitrogen dioxide is a significant pollutant that damages lungs. Wildlife thrived in cities like Venice. It happened within a month or so, telling us we can act if we need to, and the response can be rapid.

Change can happen. But perhaps the best chance we have of saving the planet is to listen to children. A remarkable increase in awareness has happened with a wave of protests all over the world. The young climate-change activist Greta Thunberg sat in front of the Swedish parliament building to protest for more action on climate change. A month later she announced that she would protest every Friday until the government changed its policy. She called the protest Fridays For Future, and it has become a global movement. The UK-based Extinction Rebellion is a non-violent protest group worried about the threat of mass extinction happening because of climate change. The movement has grown to 150,000 people in 156 different countries. In 2022, young activists from Just Stop Oil threw tomato soup over Vincent van Gogh's *Sunflowers* at the National Gallery in London. Other climate protesters threw mashed potatoes at a Claude Monet painting and smeared cake on the *Mona Lisa*. The protesters said the stunts were designed as a wake-up call in the face of a climate catastrophe. 'People are starving, people are freezing, people are dying,' one of the activists said. 'Does it take mashed potatoes on a painting to make you listen?' Protests like these are controversial, and not everyone agrees with them. Those in favour believe it's more important to make people sit up and take notice. What these protests have going for them is the number of young people involved. Lots of new and different people are getting together to protest about the problem. Let's hope for all our sakes it has an impact.

There isn't much political support for these changes. They often involve short-term pain for long-term gain – and if a politician wants to be re-elected, they don't want to annoy their voters. And the super rich and powerful often ignore the problem, because they're either too old to care, or they figure their money will insulate them from climate chaos. Billionaires like Elon Musk might plan to jet off to Mars when the going gets tough, but for the vast majority of people that's not an option.

The bottom line: We can turn this supertanker around before it's too late. If we don't, the world will be a totally different place in 50 years' time. We evolved here on Earth over millions of years. We can't sit back and give up on our planet. Instead, let's get to work.

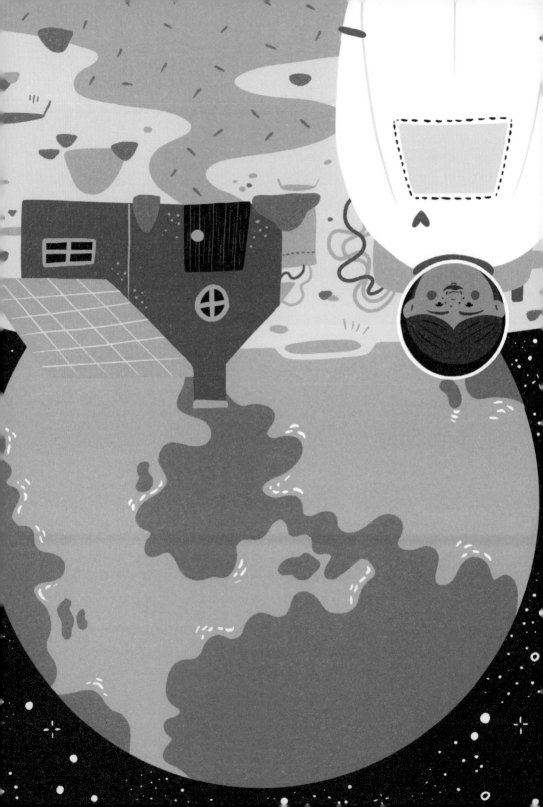

CHAPTER 12

ARE
WE
ALONE
IN THE
UNIVERSE?

P ICTURE THE SCENE. It's a quiet morning in a small rural town when a metal cylinder from Mars crashes to Earth. It lies cooling and smoking as a curious crowd gathers. The top of the container begins to slowly unscrew, and a tentacled beast with oily brown skin and huge eyes emerges. Suddenly, a blinding flash of light comes from the cylinder and people begin to burst into flames. More cylinders take flight from Mars and crash to Earth. There is widespread panic as the Martians begin to destroy cities and towns using their advanced technology. Huge fighting machines stomp across the land and cause death and destruction. The army fights back but is overwhelmed, so people are forced to hide in cellars and ruins, scavenging for food and supplies. All seems lost, humanity has been beaten. Until – for no apparent reason, the Martians start to die off. Their fighting machines are left empty, and slowly, people begin to emerge from the rubble. What brought about their end? Something the aliens had no defence against: the smallest, most humble thing on Earth – bacteria.[1]

This is a pretty great story. It's called *The War of the Worlds* and it was written by H.G. Wells in 1898. It has been adapted many times, as films, a musical and most recently in 2005 as a terrible movie starring Tom Cruise. It's such a great story because it feels real, like something that could actually happen. In fact, when it was performed on the radio in 1938, some listeners panicked, believing that an alien invasion was really happening. It wasn't, of course. But could it ever be real? Could aliens with advanced

---

1 As scientists, we must strive for accuracy and point out that viruses are even smaller than bacteria. But the truth never got in the way of a good story.

technology ever visit Earth? Is there life on other planets? Are we alone in the universe?

MARS ATTACKS

We've always been fascinated by Mars. It's one of our closest neighbours and it's a very stylish red colour. By the time Wells wrote *The War of the Worlds*, people had been observing Mars through telescopes for three centuries. Galileo discovered the planet's phases in 1610 and in 1666 Mars's polar ice caps were identified. In 1878, an Italian astronomer observed a network of straight lines across the planet which he called *canali* (Italian for 'channels'). This was mistranslated into English as 'canals', which suggested that someone had intentionally built them. The theory was that the Martians had built canals to bring water down from the polar caps to the dry land. *The War of the Worlds* was written around this time, so it's no surprise that H.G. Wells gave his Martians high-tech fighting machines and heat rays. But by the early twentieth century, better astronomical observations revealed the 'canals' were just an optical illusion, and modern high-resolution mapping of the Martian surface by spacecraft shows no channels or canals. The probes that have landed there since discovered a lifeless world too cold for water to hang about in its liquid state.

But recent missions to Mars have found exciting evidence that life could have existed in the past. Just after landing, the *Curiosity* rover found evidence of liquid water: smooth, rounded pebbles that likely rolled downstream in a deep river. It also found the remains of dried-up lakes and rivers in an area called Gale crater. The *Curiosity* rover found that ancient Mars had the right chemistry to support living things. Sulphur, nitrogen, oxygen, phosphorus and carbon – key ingredients necessary for life – were found in a powdered mud sample. So while we're unlikely to stumble over a heat ray, Mars could be a hotbed of life in a few million years. On the scale of the universe, that's no time at all.

Where else might we look for life in our solar system? One recent candidate where life might exist or have existed is the moon Enceladus, which orbits Saturn. Enceladus is so far away that if you were to get into your car one night and drive upwards at 50 km per hour it would take 3,000 years to get there. You'd better bring a flask of coffee and some sandwiches. In a combined NASA/European Space Agency mission, the *Cassini* probe left Earth in 1997 and travelled the 1.272 billion miles to Enceladus, arriving on 1 July 2004. This was a huge achievement. To get there as quickly as possible *Cassini* had to do four slingshots: two around Venus, one around Earth and one around Jupiter.

Enceladus is a world encased in ice, with an ocean of salty water hidden beneath its surface. Astronomers had observed jets of steam breaking through the ice and wondered what was in them. *Cassini* found out that it was water vapour and a mixture of organic chemicals that make up the building blocks of life. It also found free hydrogen. This is a great source of energy: the kind of energy plants make from sunlight in photosynthesis, and the kind of energy mitochondria use to power our cells. This caused a huge amount of excitement, as not only would the building blocks of life be possible, but free energy would also be present to drive everything forward. After all, life is just a bag of chemicals that can copy itself time after time with a source of energy, and if it managed this on Earth, why not somewhere else?

ALIEN ENCOUNTERS

If life *does* exist somewhere out there, has it ever popped by Earth to say hello? Throughout history, there have been reports of unidentified flying objects, or UFOs. Perhaps the first written mention came in 218 BCE when the historian Livy wrote in detail about 'phantom ships seen gleaming in the sky'. Pliny the Elder wrote about his encounter with what may have been a UFO (but was probably a meteor). 'We have an account of a spark falling from a star, and increasing as it approached the earth, until it became the size of the moon, shining as though through a cloud; it afterwards returned into the heavens.'[2] In 1561, in the German city of Nuremberg, residents saw what they described as some kind of

---

2 Remember from Chapter 2 that Pliny the Elder also believed you could cure most illnesses using dung.

battle in the sky. Objects shaped like spears, triangles, cylinders, spheres, crosses and moons darted about, crashing into each other, until a huge bang brought an end to the spectacle. Scientists think this was most likely a natural phenomenon called a 'sundog', where the sun's light is bent by ice in the atmosphere, making it look like there are multiple moving suns in the sky. Scientists: ruining the fun since 1561.

It wasn't until the age of technology that sightings of UFOs really took off. At the beginning of the twentieth century, reports of zeppelin airships in the sky began to increase, along with sightings of rockets and missiles. The town of Roswell in New Mexico became famous in 1947 after reports that a flying object had crash-landed in a field. A number of supposed witnesses said they saw the military take away a flying disc and the bodies of aliens. Since then, reports of UFOs in the skies crop up every couple of years – flying saucers, unexplained lights, alien craft. Many people claim to have been kidnapped by these mystery spaceships and experimented on.[3] Sadly, there's probably a logical explanation for all of these incidents. Most have been identified as either bright stars, comets, aircraft, space debris, balloons, natural phenomena, or just plain hoaxes.

What's more, it doesn't make much sense that an alien species would come to Earth just to sightsee. For one thing, there's distance.

---

3 Many people also claim to be Elvis Presley, the Emperor Napoleon, and Jesus Christ himself.

Although it sounds like a measurement of time, a light year is actually the *distance* light travels in one Earth year. Of course, the rest of the universe has no idea what an Earth year is, so astronomers instead use astronomical units, abbreviated AU. One AU is the distance from our sun to Earth's orbit, which is about 150 million kilometres. They also use parsecs, or parallax seconds, which are a bit more complex. They are to do with the way nearby stars appear to move in relation to more distant objects – an effect called parallax – because as our planet moves, our viewpoint changes. One parsec is 3.26 light years or roughly 31 trillion kilometres.[4] Our galaxy, the Milky Way, is more than 31,000 parsecs across, which is pretty massive.

Leaving out our own solar system, the closest planet is Proxima Centauri B, which is just four light years away from Earth. Even if we hopped aboard the *Parker Solar Probe*, which is currently the fastest object ever built (at 690,000 km/h or 0.064 per cent the speed of light) it would still take 1,500 years to travel one light year. And that's just the closest planet. The furthest star from us is Earendel, which was discovered in 2022 by the Hubble Space Telescope. It is the earliest and most distant known star, at a distance of 28 billion light years. While an alien civilisation might have developed much more advanced travel than us, one of the universe's laws is that nothing can travel faster than the speed of light. Any way you look at it, it's a long, long, *long* way to go. And then, when you get there, what you

---

4   In *Star Wars: A New Hope*, Han Solo boasts about how his ship, the *Millennium Falcon*, 'made the Kessel Run in less than 12 parsecs.' This of course doesn't make sense, as a parsec is a unit of distance, not time. The minds behind Star Wars tried to fix this in the film *Solo* by claiming that the ship did the Kessel Run in the shortest possible *distance* – 12 parsecs. Nice try.

were looking at might not be there any more – remember, it takes light one Earth year to travel through space, so what you're seeing is what a star looked like years and years ago. It could have since collapsed, or exploded, or been eaten by a giant space monster. When you look into a sky full of stars, you're actually looking back in time.

Another reason we haven't had extra-terrestrial visitors may be the age of the universe. If the universe was a 24-hour clock, humans have only been around for less than one minute. The chances of there being a civilisation close to Earth that a) developed the technology for interstellar travel at b) the exact time that we happened to be around for them to visit is extremely, extremely low. We have had the technology capable of reaching out to other stars for only about a century, just a tiny fraction of our Earth's history. The odds are more than 10 million to one that another planet is at precisely the same point in its own development.

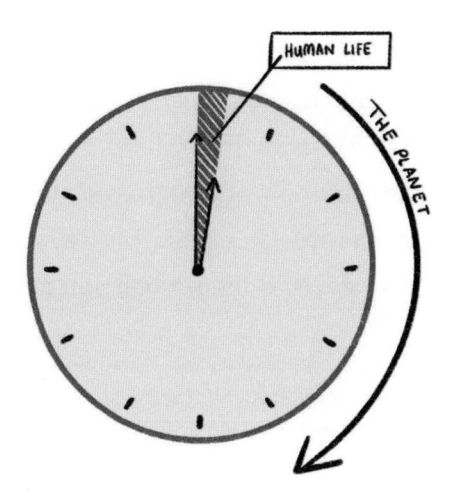

Another interesting question is what the aliens might hear if they were listening out for something. Radio broadcasts are made up of radio waves that leave Earth at the speed of light. This means that from a distance of one light year from Earth, you would hear radio that left Earth one year ago. A website called www.lightyear.fm lets you scroll back away from Earth to see what a galactic listener might hear. From a distance of fifty light years, an alien could hear 'Hey Jude' by the Beatles. More than a hundred light years away, before radio was invented? Silence.[5]

But we have recently changed to digital rather than analogue signals. Digital transmissions are far less powerful and will be much harder to detect. Earth might only have been a noisy neighbour for less than a century, a tiny blip in intergalactic time. So a space-travelling alien race might have passed by quite recently – they just didn't know we were there.

PLAYING THE GALACTIC ODDS

All this might seem a bit disappointing. Extra-terrestrial beings might be too far, too old, too young or too busy to notice us. But that doesn't mean they aren't out there. For starters, our own Milky Way galaxy contains at least 100 billion stars, and current estimates

---

5 In 1896, radio pioneer Guglielmo Marconi sent a brief transmission across a short distance. The message was his voice, saying 'CAN YOU HEAR ME'. This transmission wouldn't have been powerful enough to make it very far into space, but imagine if we received a one-word response: 'YES'.

say that there could be 6 billion Earth-like planets orbiting within their sun's habitable zones. And that's only planets that are similar to Earth – elsewhere, life could have evolved under very different conditions.

In 1961, astrophysicist Frank Drake wondered just how likely this is. He came up with an equation to calculate the odds of there being extra-terrestrial life, based on factors like: how often stars form, how often they have Earth-like planets, how many might be suitable for life, how many might be suitable for *intelligent* life, how many might transmit signals and how long they might transmit them for. This became known as the Drake equation.[6] The problem is that solving this equation involves a lot of educated guesses – we can't possibly know the correct figures for some of these factors. The SETI Institute (the Search for Extra-Terrestrial Intelligence) has been working on it for about fifty years, and they still haven't figured it out.

We can probably say that the answer to the Drake equation is somewhere between these two statements:

1. Life is very rare and Earth is a special case.
2. Life is incredibly common and Earth isn't special at all.

Now, that isn't very exact. But most scientists come down closer to number 2 above: life is incredibly common across the universe – we just haven't found it yet.

---

6 If you want to know what the whole equation looks like (some people are strange like that), it's: $N = R_* \times f_p \times n_e \times f_l \times f_i \times f_c \times L$. Easy as π!

But that brings up another question: If it's so likely that life exists out there, where the hell is everyone?! This is what's known as the Fermi paradox. Many thinkers have come up with suggestions as to why this is the case. One of these is the zoo hypothesis (or theory). This suggests that technologically advanced aliens *are* out there, but they have chosen not to contact Earth. Instead, they have somehow arranged things so that our planet is shielded from them by one-way bars. They can observe us, but we can't observe them, like animals at the zoo. They might have done this for a number of reasons:

1. Out of respect for independent and natural planetary evolution[7]
2. Because they have seen that we tend to be violent and destructive
3. They're running experiments on us, just like we use lab rats, and don't want to interfere.

This seems like a neat solution to the Fermi paradox. If the zoo hypothesis is correct, then it's understandable that we haven't found signals from space. We're just animals, pacing around our cages while the extra-terrestrials keep watch. But other scientists say this is unlikely, and is an example of anthropomorphism – our tendency to make everything about ourselves. The universe doesn't revolve around us, after all, despite what our mammies might think. The most likely answer is probably what was explained above – the sheer distance and time frame of the universe.

---

7 In the world of *Star Trek*, this is known as the 'prime directive'. It forbids spacefaring members of the Federation doing anything that might interfere with other cultures or civilisations, even if that interference is well meant.

Hopefully, what Douglas Adams wrote in *The Hitchhiker's Guide to the Galaxy* doesn't come to pass. In this book, a fleet of spaceships from the Galactic Hyperspace Planning Council arrives to orbit Earth. Through a loudspeaker, they announce that the Earth is being destroyed to make way for a hyperspatial express route through the star system. When the people of Earth are understandably shocked by this, the aliens tell them that the plans have been available to see on Alpha Centauri for fifty years, and it's now too late to make a complaint. Two minutes later, the demolition beams activate and the Earth is destroyed. A cheery thought.

The bottom line: When it comes to space, we've already made giant leaps for humankind. But we'll keep striving and learning and exploring, because while there might not be little green aliens in every neighbourhood, the truth is out there – somewhere.

CHAPTER 13

WHAT HAVE WE GOT TO LOOK FORWARD TO?

HEN I WAS a boy, I really wanted a jetpack. I'd seen one in a cartoon called *The Jetsons* where Elroy spent most of his time floating around in one. I used to imagine jetpacking my way to school. I really believed that I might get one in the future. My father (who was born in 1921) used to tell me how when he was a boy there were no jet planes and, unimaginably for me, he grew up with no television. I used to think that when I grew up and had kids, I would tell them how, unbelievably, in my own childhood there were no jetpacks – and no mobile phones. I have told them about that last one and they still refuse to believe me. Sadly, jetpacks have yet to become commonplace.

But most of all I thought the future would be like *Star Trek*. *Star Trek* was a TV series first broadcast in 1966. It followed the voyages of the crew of the starship USS *Enterprise*, a space exploration vessel built by the United Federation of Planets in the twenty-third century. Their mission was 'to explore strange new worlds, to seek out new life and new civilisations, to boldly go where no man has gone before'.

Science fiction like *The Jetsons* and *Star Trek* tried to imagine a future where daily life looked very different. To predict our own future, it's worth looking at these stories a bit more closely. Perhaps surprisingly, science fiction can help governments and corporations plan ahead. The French government have set up the Defence Innovation Agency, which has a team of science fiction writers proposing scenarios for the future. The engineering firm Arup have commissioned writers to describe four scenarios that might happen as a result of climate change. Google, Microsoft and Apple all employ science-fiction writers as consultants. For businesses, science fiction can free up the mind. Science fiction can inspire people who work in the technology sector to come up with new products and services. Motorola said it was the hand-held wireless communicators used in *Star Trek* that motivated them to make the first mobile phone. Amazon's Alexa voice assistant was inspired by the talking computer on the Starship *Enterprise*. The Kindle was inspired by an electronic book that featured in a novel by Neal Stephenson. The future as seen in sci-fi might seem far away, but technology is bringing us closer each day.

UP AND AWAY

The spacecraft in *Star Trek* have a key technology – the warp drive – which allows them to travel at speeds faster than light. Sadly, the only means of space transport that we now have is rocket propulsion, which hasn't changed much since the 1960s. This means space travel is constrained by chemistry. Burning combustible fuel with storable or cryogenic oxidisers remains the only way to boost rockets. The reason we don't have jetpacks is similar – the amount of fuel needed to get a (thick, heavy) human off the ground just isn't feasible. The jet itself would also be extremely dangerous to other fliers –

to say nothing of the flames shooting out – and it would probably be uncomfortably loud and awkward.

Even though we mightn't have warp speed or jetpacks, a lot is happening when it comes to flying through the air. Electric aeroplanes are being developed, with more powerful batteries and lighter, more powerful engines, which are less harmful to the environment.[1] It's likely that self-driving aeroplanes will become more of a reality as artificial intelligence is used to fly, although a fully pilotless aeroplane isn't on the cards yet. Electric flying taxis are being considered, which may eventually lead to a future out of *The Jetsons* – flying cars in the skies of cities. Solar-powered airships are also being developed and may usher in an era of slow travel. An airship would take 44 hours to cross the Atlantic. Imagine the views!

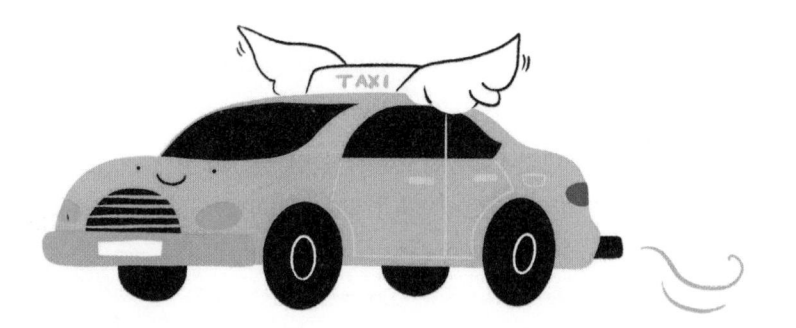

One of the more outlandish ideas is to build an orbital ring around the Earth. This would involve a strong steel cable about 80 km above the Earth. It would rotate, creating a force. Two magnetic levitation (Maglev) train tracks on the underside of the

---

1 Flying is a big contributor to climate change. If the aviation industry was a country, it would rank among the worst countries in the world for carbon dioxide emissions.

ring would transport passengers at incredible speeds. It is currently thought that a Maglev on an orbital ring would allow passengers to get to Australia from Europe in 45 minutes.

Space travel is also on the up and up, if you'll pardon the pun. The International Space Station has been called 'Starfleet in gestation'. The next step is the lunar gateway, which is planned for 2026. It will orbit the moon and allow astronauts to return to the moon's surface. Elon Musk's company SpaceX became the first to deliver cargo to the International Space Station in 2012. Jeff Bezos's spaceflight company, Blue Origin, is also in the rocket development business. In October 2021, William Shatner (age 90), the actor who played Captain Kirk on the original *Star Trek* series, boarded a Blue Origin capsule and successfully flew to space, becoming the oldest person to do so. The next big frontier is to get a spaceship to Mars – NASA are aiming to safely deliver humans there by 2030.

FUTURE LIVING

Another key sci-fi technology is machines that can create something out of nothing at the touch of a button. In *Star Trek,* replicators were used to create everything from food to goods and even oxygen, while the Jetsons could order dinner through their futuristic food-making machine. Three-dimensional (3D) printing technologies might be getting us closer to this reality. Traditional production involves cutting away materials to make the final product, while 3D printing adds layers of material to build something new. It is

being used to make food, including chocolate, crackers, pasta and plant-based meat substitutes. It can also produce clothes, medical prosthetics, and even components for cars, planes and boats. It is likely to advance even further, with proposals to print whole houses and their contents. Who knows where it might lead – an end to world hunger, or just an endless supply of Lego bricks?

What about medical advances? One *Star Trek* character, Geordi La Forge, wears a visor that enables him to see, despite being blind from birth. A device somewhat similar to the visor has been invented. In 2005 a team at Stanford University used a combination of a microchip implanted behind the retina of a mouse and goggles with LED read-outs linked to a small camera that allowed mice to distinguish black from white. This device was then used by a woman who had lost her sight in a car crash, which allowed her to see object outlines and differences in light intensity. But we are some way off a device like Geordi's.

Injections in *Star Trek* are given by 'hypospray', which doesn't involve a needle and can be used through clothing. The FDA recently approved a device that can use ultrasonic waves to open pores in the skin, allowing liquids, including vaccines, to be injected without needles. A device with a high-pressure jet is also being developed, which is being tested as a way to deliver vaccines in powdered form. This will mean no injections for vaccines and no need to keep vaccines at a low temperature to preserve them, which is an issue in the developing world. And no more sore arms!

In *The Jetsons*, a doctor assesses patients using videoconferencing technology. This became common during the COVID-19 pandemic.

People could see a doctor while staying safe in their own homes. *Star Trek: Voyager* has an emergency hologram doctor who is an expert in all fields of medicine. We are a long way off robotic doctors, although there are robots that can perform some types of surgery. In diagnosis, artificial intelligence is being used more often, most recently in the diagnosis of breast cancer, where the technology did better than humans. Ultimately, it may well be a computer that will diagnose illness and provide treatment.

We can anticipate a large amount of progress in what medicine will look like in the future. Vast amounts of money and resources are currently being spent on medical research and the effort to develop new medicines, as we saw in Chapter 2. There is no doubt that we will continue to see tremendous progress. Trials are under way, with a range of approaches being tested, including more recent technologies such as gene therapy, which involves replacing a faulty gene that is causing a specific disease. I predict that we will look back on the main diseases that kill us nowadays (cancer and heart disease) as diseases of the past, with many of us living into old age and afflicted by fewer diseases. We will all die one day, and may eventually fade gracefully away, having lived a long and hopefully prosperous and fulfilled life.

What about the holodeck, which has been invented by the time of *Star Trek: The Next Generation*? This lets people enter into virtual reality – a simulated situation that looks and feels real. Imagine if that came true? We could all end up living virtual lives. This technology is getting closer, driven mainly by the gaming industry, but businesses are also interested. Wall-to-wall high-depth monitors, sophisticated projectors, motion sensors and other technologies are being announced every day. There are virtual or augmented reality headsets (such as Facebook's Oculus Rift and Sony's PSVR2), but the design isn't lightweight or comfortable to use for long.[2] There is a program called Walk on Mars that allows you to – you guessed it – walk on Mars, using real-life images captured by the Mars rover *Perseverance*. While the holodeck is still some way off, this technology is still letting us explore space, even if it is from our own living rooms.

But a lot of sci-fi technologies are closer to reality. Automatic sliding doors first appeared in *Star Trek*, but they were operated with ropes. These are now used almost everywhere. *Star Trek* also had hand-held touchscreen 'data slates' known as personal access display devices (PADDs), which we now use in the form of iPads and tablets. The universal translator was able to scan brain waves to interpret unknown languages into the user's own language. There are many apps that allow us to have conversations with others, using real-time translators. Some headphones can now translate a foreign language directly into your ears. This is like the famous Babel Fish in Douglas Adams's *The Hitchhiker's Guide to the Galaxy*, but in that case, it was an actual fish that had to be stuck into your ear!

---

2 Motion sickness can be a problem with VR headsets. The brain thinks that it is moving through space, but the body knows that it isn't. The most common symptoms are general discomfort, eye strain, headache, nausea, vomiting, sweating, drowsiness, disorientation and apathy. Who's first up?

Perhaps it will be in robotics that we will see the biggest advances in the coming decade. Data is the name of the robot in *Star Trek: The Next Generation*. He is a synthetic life form with artificial intelligence, whose brain allows him to be self-aware. In his early years he had trouble understanding various aspects of human behaviour and was unable to feel emotion. In *The Jetsons*, Rosie the Robot Maid rolls around and keeps the house tidy. When at home by herself, she functions as a house sitter and security system. She thinks romance is a waste of time, but eventually falls in love with a robotic filing cabinet.

We are a long way off a Data or Rosie, although a lot of research is being done on robotics. In 2018, $4.9 billion in venture capital investment (putting money into new projects) was made in 400 separate deals in the USA. A similar amount has been invested in

China. But an Irish robot got a lot of attention in 2019. Robotics engineers from Trinity College Dublin unveiled a robot called Stevie II, described as Ireland's first socially assistive robot with advanced artificial intelligence. Stevie II is for use in long-term care environments for the elderly and for people living with disabilities. The team consulted with a range of experts, including nurses and caregivers, when they were developing Stevie II. ALONE, the charity that supports older people in Ireland, is a key partner. Stevie II is now being tested in care homes in the USA and UK. His initial jobs were to remind residents when to take their medication. He can also help with video calls. He can recognise faces and voices and has turned out to be a big hit with residents, who enjoy the conversations they have with him. His inventors have said that a key goal for future development is to enable Stevie II to engage in small talk or the craic, which will make him truly Irish.

WRONG TURNS

When it comes to predicting the future, science fiction can also be a lesson in not getting too cocky. The famous sci-fi writer Jules Verne wrote influential novels like *Journey to the Centre of the Earth* and *Twenty Thousand Leagues Under the Sea*. Verne mentions several crazy concepts for the time – what we'd one day call the submarine, space travel, the jukebox and the holograph. While Verne was right about a lot of amazing things in his books, he wasn't perfect. In fact, he was terribly wrong about how we'd get to the moon. He claimed we'd shoot people into space from a big gun. Obviously, we aren't journeying to the centre of the Earth anytime soon either.

In 1929, Irish scientist J.D. Bernal wrote a book with the exciting title of *The World, the Flesh and the Devil*. He predicted a small sense organ with enhanced vision and hearing that could detect wireless frequencies. With this wireless sense, humans would be able to communicate with each other across vast distances. This was his version of the World Wide Web. But he didn't predict the computer as the main technological development of the twentieth century. This was partly because, at that time, computers (and they weren't even called that then) were run on punch cards.

Similarly, the makers of *The Jetsons* imagined the future to be a suburban 1960s American family – but in the air. George goes to work in a spaceship, while Jane goes shopping in the sky. The two children go to a floating high school. When Jane goes shopping, she uses green cash bills – not a plastic credit card, and certainly not a mobile phone or smartwatch. George sits at his futuristic-shaped desk, but he works with pen and paper rather than a laptop. The TV show didn't predict the arrival of electronic computers or that we would be able to carry them in our pockets.

This, of course, gives us a warning. If sci-fi missed key technologies which have had such a major effect on our lives, what else are we missing? And what about COVID-19? Although scientists had predicted another pandemic, nobody anticipated that. We're only now coming to terms with what COVID-19 might mean for the future. Who knows what other blind spots we might have?

PLANETARY TIMELINE

But there are some things that we can predict with a reasonable amount of certainty, based on where we are now and the speed of progress. A website called FutureTimeline.net has mapped out a timeline of what might happen over the remainder of this century. The starting point is how the world is now. So what's coming down the line for planet Earth?

In the 2020s, climate change will likely become more and more of a concern and will begin to threaten food and water supplies. Cheap, 3D-printed clothes will appear, getting rid of sweatshops, but many people will also lose their jobs.

The 2030s will finally see a substantial shift towards renewable energy supplies because of breakthroughs in nanotechnology, which will make these supplies cheaper and more efficient. Nuclear fusion will also be used more and more as a source of energy.

In the 2040s, genetics, nanotechnology and robotics will become more advanced. Devices will be implanted into the human body to help combat disease, enhance our senses, allow for different forms of communication and provide entertainment. There will be colonies on Mars and on the moon. Artificial intelligence will play a much bigger role in how businesses and governments make decisions and will take over human decision-making.

By 2060, the world's population will have reached a plateau and will start to decline. By the 2070s, a full-scale environmental catastrophe will have happened, because in spite of our best efforts, climate change has still been occurring. Large-scale evacuations of cities will have happened because of rising sea levels.

By the 2080s, though, scientific discovery will massively accelerate because of artificial intelligence. Conventional meat from animals will be completely phased out. Androids will be used in law enforcement.

By the 2090s, *Homo sapiens* is no longer the dominant species on earth. The day-to-day running of countries will be done by ultra-fast, supremely intelligent robots and virtual entities. Most of the world's languages will no longer be in widespread use. English, Mandarin and Spanish will be the three dominant languages. The average employee will be working for less than 20 hours per week. Western Antarctica will become one of the fastest-developing regions in the world. It will have a climate similar to Alaska today, the ice caps there will have melted and immigration from regions damaged by climate change will be encouraged. The cities there will become artistic melting pots with hugely diverse populations.

By the turn of the twenty-second century, the world will be almost unrecognisable. How do you think that future sounds? Be excited – you may well live to see it.

A CURIOUS FUTURE

We humans are a curious species. Our curiosity led us to invent science and we began to find out fascinating things about the world we live in, which only made us more curious. We continue to make discoveries at an incredible rate, helped by the machines we invented, especially in the past ten years or so as the digital age has taken off. I'd love to move through time to the future and see how many of the things I've covered here will have become true because of science. As yet, a time machine hasn't been invented, although according to some physicists that is not completely beyond the bounds of possibility.[3] Until we master that, time will keep moving forward, bringing us into a brave new world. It is up to all of us to make sure that the future is as good as we can possibly make it.

The bottom line: As the cosmologist and science communicator Carl Sagan once said: 'Somewhere, something incredible is waiting to be known.'

---

3 It involves that most famous of equations, Einstein's $E=MC^2$, which suggests that time goes slower where there is less gravity. Astronauts come back to Earth a fraction of a second younger than when they left – they've time-travelled into the future. But to travel for more than a millisecond, we would need to build a spacecraft that can reach close to the speed of light, which – at 299,792,458 metres per second – is pretty nippy.

INDEX